Michael Winterbottom: Interviews

Conversations with Filmmakers Series
Gerald Peary, General Editor

Michael Winterbottom
INTERVIEWS

Edited by Damon Smith

University Press of Mississippi / Jackson

www.upress.state.ms.us

The University Press of Mississippi is a member of the Association
of American University Presses.

First printing 2011
∞

Library of Congress Cataloging-in-Publication Data

Winterbottom, Michael.
  Michael Winterbottom : interviews / edited by Damon Smith.
      p. cm. — (Conversations with filmmakers series)
  Includes index.
  Includes filmography.
  ISBN 978-1-60473-840-7 (cloth : alk. paper)—ISBN 978-1-60473-841-4 (ebook)
  ISBN 978-1-4968-5802-3 (paperback)
  1. Winterbottom, Michael—Interviews. 2. Motion picture producers and directors—
United States—Interviews. I. Smith, Damon. II. Title.
  PN1998.3.W5685A5 2010
  791.4302'33092—dc22
  [B]   2010024578

British Library Cataloging-in-Publication Data available

Contents

Introduction

Within minutes of meeting Michael Winterbottom, even the savviest journalist learns one thing about the affable, boyishly handsome British filmmaker: he doesn't like to be pigeonholed. Asked a personal question, he demurs. Loath to psychologize his characters or intellectualize the artistry behind his craft, Winterbottom often reverts to the plainest language he can find to address questions about style and motivation. "It's just a story that interests me," might be the commonest refrain of the interviews gathered in this book, regardless of whether they appeared in mainstream newspapers or highbrow film journals. It isn't that Winterbottom is willfully evasive or contemptuous of the newsmedia discussion format. Quite the contrary: he's consistently garrulous and enthusiastic when speaking to the press, quick to laugh and brandish his Lancastrian wit, always conscientious about elucidating what he can, within certain limits, without ever coming off as overearnest or self-absorbed. Though fluent in literature, world politics, and film history, his responses tend to focus on describing the work at hand, the technical process and actual circumstances in which his cinema is created, rather than the big ideas or social issues they engage. It's as if he worries that prattling on about sociopolitical themes and deeper layers of meaning will overwhelm what for him is absolutely essential: the stories, the relationship between characters, the sense of lives being lived onscreen. And for all his restless energy, expressed as much in his light-speed conversational style as in the pace, breadth, and scope of his prodigious and notably eclectic artistic output, traits only the rare interviewer fails to mention, Winterbottom prefers to keep things simple, as authentic as possible.

One of the first times we met, shortly after he finished shooting his big-budget period Western The Claim, he remarked in an interview included in this volume (Smith 2000), "If you have dreams as a director, you don't want to be worried about how your dreams will be interpreted. If you're having the dream, you don't necessarily want to be analyzing them. I don't start off with a particular end product or message in mind, or feeling like I must do a film now that exposes things, or that is more political or more social. I look for the logic of the story to point the way toward how the film should be made." Winterbottom's propensity for keeping things simple in his approach—working with small crews, available light, handheld digital cameras, radio mics, and minuscule budgets—belies the dramatic complexity and often disorienting kineti-cism of his films, which are firmly rooted in the dizzying milieu of the varied locations he shoots in. Apart from the docu-realist authenticity these techniques afford in capturing the specificity of place, which have come to define his preferred working mode from *Wonderland* on down to *A Mighty Heart* and *Genova*, they also allow him to work with fewer constraints than most filmmakers. He'd rather be out in the streets than locked on a studio lot surrounded by people and lighting equipment, or waiting for line producers to cordon off public spaces and then coordi-nate masses of extras. The fewer the limitations and barriers, the more immediate and visceral his films become too, and the happier he is, a point he returns to again and again in these interviews. No wonder so many of his movies (*Butterfly Kiss*, *Welcome to Sarajevo*, *In This World*, *The Road to Guantánamo*) have taken the form of a road journey.

Early in his career, Winterbottom explained to *Time Out*'s Geoff An-drew some of the basic underlying principles of his first feature film, *Butterfly Kiss*, the story of two wayward young women on a killing spree, set along nondescript highways in northeast England: "We liked the idea of a British road movie, which is so anachronistic it's a terrible idea. In Britain, you don't have that same sense of journey, of freedom, as you do in America. But *Butterfly Kiss* is about people going round and round, not going anywhere; everywhere looks the same, clogged with traffic. Miriam and Eunice don't even have cars—half the time they're walking along the side of the road! At the same time, it's also a movie specifically set in the north-east, but we wanted to get away from those images of red-brick towns and beautiful dales. It's the anonymity of the place that matters here." Though brief, the comment illuminates some of Winterbottom's principal concerns as a filmmaker: the conflict be-tween freedom and displacement, the attention to everyday detail, and the desire to move beyond conventional depictions of familiar places. Winterbottom's strict adherence to a strain of realism, his desire to keep his mode of representation "one step away from the real," as he remarks to Alex Fitch, extends as much to the kinds of experiential stories he often tells about the impact of war, immigration, separation, and cultural dislocation as it does to the aesthetic mashup of textures (stock footage, DV, 16mm) that mark films as diverse in tone and geography as *Welcome to Sarajevo* and *24 Hour Party People*, a fictionalized portrait of the Madchester music scene.

Certainly, Winterbottom's background in television work as an assistant editor at Thames Television and short-term apprenticeship with Lindsay Anderson played a key role in the development of his methodology and generally skeptical attitude toward industrial modes of film production. In Europe, television is the staging ground for many young feature-film directors, and Winterbottom built his reputation with early made-for-TV dramas like *Forget About Me*, *Love Lies Bleeding*, and *Under the Sun*. He also established important working relationships in this medium with long-term collaborators like screenwriter Frank Cottrell Boyce, editor Trevor Waite, and BBC producer Andrew Eaton, with whom he co-founded Revolution Films in 1994 after the tremendous success of their four-part series *Family*, written by Roddy Doyle. Eaton would go on to produce nearly every feature film Winterbottom directed. In his lengthy interview with Michel Ciment and Yann Tobin of *Positif* (1996), translated into English for the first time here, Winterbottom reflects back on this time, marveling at the surprising amount of freedom he had to pursue projects that interested him, on budgets that were modest but enough to get the job done. He also speaks about some of his formative experiences growing up ("The television was always on; this was how I discovered not only old films, but also the young English directors of the seventies, like Ken Loach and Mike Leigh"), as well as his admiration for Swedish maestro Ingmar Bergman, about whom he directed two documentaries for Channel Four over a six-month period: "I really became passionate, not only for Bergman's oeuvre, in its immensity and diversity, but especially for his way of working."

Although some critics have noted a formal connection between *Butterfly Kiss* and Bergman's *Persona*, in the sense of two women's identities merging, there is no abiding stylistic correspondence between the two filmmakers, given the latter's sharp emphasis on fantasy and psychological reality. For Winterbottom, it was Bergman's work ethic that left the deepest impression, a position he clarified when he spoke to Roy Frumkes from *Films in Review*, who asked about the early docs: "What's great about someone who has a career like Bergman's is that he worked constantly over a long period of time, and you can get to the point where you can see phases in his work, see themes come back and change. There's actually enough volume that if he does a comedy that doesn't succeed, it's merely a blip in the overall work. You tend to associate Bergman with those chamber pieces like *The Seventh Seal*, and then you realize that those really began in the sixties, and he'd already been making films for twenty years. There's that kind of longevity. Some years he'd make two films in a summer. It was a great situation and one that is practically impossible to achieve." Bergman's cultivation of a small group of collaborators, most of whom Winterbottom interviewed for *The Magic Lantern* and *The Director*, provided a further source of inspiration for his own approach, as he tells *The Guardian*'s Simon Hattenstone: "Bergman wrote and shot fifty-five films or whatever, as well as his main career being in the theatre, and he did that because he had a small team of collaborators and there was no finance-raising whatsoever. He didn't make *Star Wars*, he made 'four actors in a room.'" Although Winterbottom speaks often in these interviews about his mentor Lindsay Anderson (Ciment and Tobin, Hattenstone, Béar, Rodrick, Smith), praising the boldness and freedom of his cinema, he confesses dismay at his hero's lack of industriousness and thirst for petty disputation, the precise opposite of Bergman's intimate, small-scale productions and indefatigable work ethic. When *Cinema Scope*'s Adam Nayman asks Winterbottom if he considers himself prolific, a question most interviewers (including myself) have been curious to ask or comment on, given the astonishing speed at which he produces new work, he replies, "It's really about working. . . . If I took a break for a couple of years, I wouldn't have anything I wanted to make a movie about. If you keep working, it gives you energy and desire to try something else."

Although Winterbottom has always been reluctant to assign any overarching thematic structure to his work, repeatedly insisting that there is no pattern other than "stories that interest me," he has had quite a lot to say over the years about Thomas Hardy's nineteenth-century novel *Jude the Obscure*, which he adapted in 1996. The book is a touchstone for Winterbottom, a talisman from his adolescence ("I must have read it four or five times," he tells Ciment and Tobin) that continues to exert a powerful influence on the shape of his worldview. Specifically, Hardy's empathy with outsiders and marginal characters like Jude, a provincial aspirant whose scholarly ambitions are dashed by elitist prejudice, left an imprint. "Here is someone who wants to change his life," Winterbottom explains to *Newsday*'s Jan Stuart, when asked why he chose to film a novel whose preoccupations with the English class system and constraints on freethinking women seem dated. "There are many who want to improve their lives but can't for whatever reason: prejudice, economic problems. . . . The nature of the prejudice may have changed, but the ostracism is often exactly the same. So it's not a question of it being particularly relevant now, but always relevant." Speaking to Jasper Rees of the *Independent* about the resonance of Jude's situation with his own background in working-class Blackburn, Winterbottom says, "When I left school, I was desperate to get out. But I think that's not to do with the place: when you're growing you feel like you want to do things and escape where you're from." One of the first in his family to go to university, he went on to take a degree in English at Oxford.

Having forged a strong social conscience in his youth, a sensibility enriched by his encounter with Hardy and to some extent the early films of Ken Loach, Winterbottom's features are populated with refugees (*Welcome to Sarajevo, In This World*), immigrants (*The Claim*), outsiders and social marginals (*Butterfly Kiss, Jude, I Want You, Code 46*), blue-collar strivers (*Wonderland, With or Without You, Go Now*), and people en route from one place to another who find themselves in a forbidding, strange, or hostile environment (*The Road to Guantánamo, Genova*). The self-admitted emphasis on "people who are excluded from society" (Ciment and Tobin) emerges consistently in the narrative treatments he's developed with Frank Cottrell Boyce and Andrew Eaton, regardless of the period or setting. Upon the release of his dystopian love story *Code 46*, for instance, Winterbottom highlighted the connective tissue between this near-future sci-fi tale and the Golden Bear–winning Afghan road movie that preceded it to indieWIRE's Wendy Mitchell: "Because Andrew and I were off making *In This World*, about two refugees, we got this idea of people having no papers and trying to travel from one place to another and the problems that creates. And a lot of that world— refugee camps, people in deserts, people outside the system, without papers, excluded—those elements are part of the social fabric of *Code 46* as well."

Never far from Winterbottom's mind when questions of politics arise are the relationships between individuals and lovers and family members in his films (see Fitch, Fraser, Mitchell, Kaufman, etc.), even when these characters' personal stories unfold within a harried, confusing real-world milieu that speaks urgently to larger sociopolitical issues like war, terrorism, or post-9/11 conflict. Throughout these conversations, he continually reframes or tactfully dodges interviewers' questions about the overt political overtones to be found in, say, *In This World* or *A Mighty Heart*, preferring to reflect instead on the humanistic dimension, and his hope that representing the harrowing experience of living through hostilities or cultural upheaval will engage audiences on a more immediate level. Describing the genesis of *Welcome to Sarajevo*, based on a Bosnian war correspondent's memoir about his adoption of a child refugee, Winterbottom expresses his discomfort with identifying himself as a "political filmmaker" to indieWIRE's Stephen Garrett, saying he simply wanted to capture what it was like to live in the war-torn city. But he does admit that his docu-realist strategy has a moral urgency: "Our hope when we made the film was that it might bring Sarajevo to the attention of people, because the starting point for making the film was a sense of the bizarreness—that here's a war happening in the middle of Europe, we're watching it on television, you can see it every day, and yet we're not doing anything about it—we're not doing anything to stop it." He reiterates the point in conversation with Liza Béar for *BOMB*: "I hope how the film works is that what the journalists feel and experience is a more acute form of what everyone can feel and experience. It's not specific to them. They're in the quandary of being right there, and not being able to do anything about it, but that's what everyone feels when they watch on TV what the journalists have witnessed firsthand."

Winterbottom has been less self-conscious about revealing the left-leaning political motivations behind the two films he's co-directed with Mat Whitecross, who initially served as his production assistant on *In This World* and then handled editing duties on *9 Songs*. In 2006, at the height of the Bush administration's war on terror, the pair collaborated on *The Road to Guantánamo*, a fiction/documentary hybrid that retraces the journey of the Tipton Three, a trio of British Pakistani youths who were detained in Afghanistan on trumped-up terror charges and shipped off to the Guantánamo Bay detention center, where they were interrogated, tortured, and then released. Winterbottom's remarks to Green-Cine's David D'Arcy are characteristically guarded at first, deflecting any inference that their purpose in making the film was to do anything more than tell "the story of just these three individuals. It's very specific. It's not a film about a general situation." Later in the exchange, Winterbottom opens up to an impressive degree and even reverses himself, stating more explicitly the rationale behind this choice of material: "What we're trying to show is that this is the routine of the system. This is not a film about the individual isolated example which is different to the general. . . . So things like stress positions, short shacklings, strobe lights, loud music, the isolation—all these things are part of what the system of Guantánamo does, which the system in Guantánamo feels is acceptable. This is just what goes on routinely in Guantánamo, and hopefully, people, when they watch the film, will think that this shouldn't happen." Winterbottom's only foray into straight documentary since his television days, also with Whitecross, was on 2009's *The Shock Doctrine*, an openly strident adaptation of Naomi Klein's book on "disaster capitalism," though it departed significantly enough from the author's theory of free-market exploitation that she distanced herself from the film shortly before it aired on More4. (She did, however, join the directors for a Q&A at the Sundance 2010 premiere.) Here again, Winterbottom speaks frankly about his political sentiments to John O'Connell at the *Times* (U.K.), expressing admiration for Klein's "simple and clever" argument, which links events in Pinochet's Chile with the privatization of war in Iraq, and airing concern about the return of "the Keynesian model."

Except for this sharp detour into polemical filmmaking, there's every reason to take Winterbottom at his word when he claims that he's more interested in people than hammering away at issues (see his comments to me in 2009 about cinema, politics, and truth-telling). For *A Mighty Heart*, he stuck very closely to the spirit of the memoir by Mariane Pearl, wife of murdered *Wall Street Journal* reporter Daniel Pearl, attempting to stay faithful to her experiences as she waited to hear news about her missing spouse, who was kidnapped by Muslim extremists in Karachi, Pakistan. He acknowledges that both *The Road to Guantánamo* and *A Mighty Heart* are about people caught up in the aftermath of 9/11, with "extreme actions on both sides." But it's the humanity at stake in such tense and perilous circumstances that attracted him to the story, more than the opportunity it may have afforded to pronounce his views on contemporary world events using one of the biggest celebrities in the world, Angelina Jolie, as his mouthpiece. "Really, the film is more about Mariane," Winterbottom tells Peter Sobczynski, "her response to the kidnapping and the news of his death, her relations to the other people in the house and their relationships to the investigation outside." Even with a Hollywood megastar in the mix, Winterbottom changed nothing about his métier, shooting on location in Pakistan and India without permits, keeping his crew setups small and intimate, crafting a scruffy, visually arresting drama that looked nothing like a studio picture. As with all Winterbottom films, *A Mighty Heart* conveyed the grit, tang, and commotion of the actual places it was filmed in. Chatting with *Electric Sheep*'s Alex Fitch, he confides, "It's fun if those areas between the story you're telling, the world where they are set and the world where you are making them, are integral and complex and have different sorts of connections with reality."

If there's one thing that interviewers have repeatedly pressed Winterbottom to speak about in the fifteen years since his first sit-down with a major publication, it's this adherence and fidelity to achieving a semblance of documentary realism. Most of the interviews included in this volume touch on this aspect of Winterbottom's process, his preference for placing actors in real situations—in cafés and clubs, out in the streets, at border crossings or in a war zone, even under the harsh climes of a Canadian winter—rather than the sterile, tightly controlled environment of studio soundstages and artificially managed outdoor sets. Several interviewers (Anthony Kaufman, David D'Arcy) have asked about the influence of the Dogme 95 manifesto on his decision to shoot, whenever possible, with natural light and handheld digital cameras, to keep the production stripped-down and nimble. "From my point of view, the smaller the crew the better, and the simpler the story the better," he tells Colin Fraser at *FILMINK*. "Hand-held cameras and natural light are good. All those things make the film even more focused on what's actually happening in front of the camera. They keep it relaxed, intimate, and enjoyable." He notes that Dogme was "a publicity stunt" valuable mostly for demonstrating to exhibitors that digital video was a viable format. For Winterbottom, there was nothing new in those protocols, which date back to the major European postwar cinema of Rossellini, Godard, Truffaut, Wenders, and Herzog. "The connection between New German Cinema, the French New Wave, and neorealism," he told me in our interview from 2000, "is the idea of people going out and trying to do things as simply as possible. Telling a story but allowing for things that are accidental and that happen by chance, so [you get] that kind of freshness those kind of films have."

Winterbottom's period films—*Jude, The Claim, 24 Hour Party People, Tristram Shandy*—have presented a significant challenge in this regard, requiring a greater degree of choreography and coordination with actors, crew, art directors, and costume designers, not to mention budgetary considerations. "I was dreading making my first costume film," he confides to Ciment and Tobin about *Jude*. "We started by looking for locations that weren't too constraining. . . . I wanted the possibility of moving freely with the actors if they changed their way of thinking or wanted to try other variations." Years later, he remarks to David D'Arcy: "I have to say that, although I've done period films, I find them quite tricky. It's not my most comfortable genre." And to *Cineaste*'s Richard Porton, who asks about the bare-bones aesthetic on *9 Songs*, he says: "Yeah, the idea now is to keep things as simple as possible. Although, with *Tristram*, you couldn't possibly have a shoot that was as simple as *9 Songs* or *Wonderland* since the period stuff demanded you have a bigger cast with more elements to choreograph and, ultimately, a bigger crew." Winterbottom's one foray into big-budget filmmaking, on *The Claim*, proved to be a source of frustration, as he avers to the *Guardian*: "It was the biggest budget I'd worked with, and the one where the shortage of money was the most problematic. In the end, we had to take twenty pages out of the script the week before we made it to try and make it shootable. It's like we can make a film at £2m and shoot the script, but at £20m we have to cut the script by twenty pages."

Both logistically and financially, the experience of making *The Claim* (which performed poorly at the box office) reinforced Winterbottom and Eaton's modus operandi of "keeping things simple," and provided fertile ground for the concept of *24 Hour Party People*, one of their most free-spirited and diverting features. Another period drama, the film revisits the golden era of Manchester's world-famous music scene of the late seventies to early nineties (Joy Division, Happy Mondays), with comic actor Steve Coogan playing Factory Records impresario Tony Wilson. *Filmmaker*'s Jeremiah Kipp caught up with Winterbottom and asked whether the quick-and-dirty digital-video aesthetic he employed in recreating the music and milieu mirrored the DIY ethos of the era. "You're certainly right that the idea was to make the film in the spirit of Factory," he replies, "which is essentially the spirit of punk—and although their music isn't punk, that was their starting point. That's what excited them enough to say, 'Fuck it! Let's all go off and do what we want to do!' Within the filming, I tried to give the actors as much a sense of that as possible. Using digital video helps, but the key in terms of how we made it was to not use any lighting really, or to only use the lights that existed within the club during those scenes. We would give each of the actors radio [microphones], allowing them to talk at the same time—with two people talking in one corner and two in the other. We'd shoot the entire scene in one go. It was that freedom that motivated us, allowing the actors to roam around and have the camera do what it wants to. That can be done on 35mm or 16mm or DV." As Winterbottom matured as a filmmaker, he settled on bringing a more liberatory energy to his craft, showing how deftly he could move between earnest working-class dramas and gritty docu-fiction, genre film and comedy, not to mention literary adaptation, another talking point in so many of these interviews.

That sense of frivolity and play, of artistic anarchy combined with an insistence on verisimilitude that's "one step away from the real," inform what many critics regard as his most ambitious undertaking, an adaptation of Laurence Sterne's classic novel *Tristram Shandy*, long regarded by scholars and experienced scriptwriters as an "unfilmable" book. Winterbottom's approach was to remain faithful to the spirit, rather than the letter, of the novel, with a farcical, semi-improvised, ad hoc narrative style that echoed Sterne's own tangential textual digressions and satirical sensibility (see Nayman, Porton, and D'Arcy). The meta aspect of *A Cock and Bull Story*—it's a film about the making of a film version of Sterne's novel, with Coogan and another real-life comedian, Rob Brydon, essentially playing exaggerated versions of themselves—fuels much of Richard Porton's dialogue with Winterbottom, who explains why it made sense to create, in Porton's words, a kind of film à clef: "Since we were on a film set making a film partially about a film set, the idea was that it was easier to borrow certain aspects of the actual shoot and incorporate these into the script. It's not that it was important for aspects of the film to be true; it was just easier to borrow things that were happening rather than generating all sorts of fictional events. So the discussion in the film about whether to include the Widow Wadman actually mirrored some actual discussions we'd had at an earlier point." Stephen Rodrick, writing for the *New York Times Magazine*, provides one of the most insightful pieces in this book with his 2005 profile, conveying an exuberant sense of life on the set of a Winterbottom film. He even found himself cast in the film—as a *Times* reporter seeking an interview.

One of the things I have tried to convey in gathering the texts for this volume is that there is a method to the genre-scrambling madness and stylistic adventurousness of Michael Winterbottom. On one hand, he's an anti-auteur, continually emphasizing that film is a "collaborative process," that there is "no pattern" to his work (Smith 2000). Winterbottom's long-term relationship with Andrew Eaton and the rest of the Revolution Films posse further attests to the open-ended spirit in which he develops projects with others, relying on their input and contributions. On the other hand, his films do bear a signature, both in terms of the conditions under which they are filmed and the sense of reality that erupts through his fictional constructs, as well as in the types of location-specific stories and characters (marginals, outsiders, "people excluded from society") that continually draw his attention. He routinely pushes boundaries and challenges the conventions of mainstream cinema, giving each film a vitality and authenticity that has nothing to do with "big, dramatic moments" (see his comments to Garrett, Kaufman, Béar, D'Arcy). The most provocative example of this trait is evident from his work on *9 Songs*, an intimate concert film-cum-sex drama that was alternately reviled and celebrated for its graphic depiction of intercourse, masturbation, oral sex, and light bondage. Denounced by conservative columnists and members of Parliament, Winterbottom cried foul on the establishment (see Rodrick, Linden, Fraser), claiming it was hypocritical to impugn representations of self-evidently "natural" acts of love, and was vindicated when the British equivalent of the MPAA declined to give the film an X rating. In fact, there is a love story at the heart of nearly every Winterbottom film, including his most recent effort, *The Killer Inside Me*, an adaptation of Jim Thompson's novel about a handsome young small-town sheriff harboring dark impulses. He is at once an old-school humanist and a trail-blazing iconoclast, attempting to tell stories with universal appeal within a framework that is anything but predictable or hidebound to tradition. As Winterbottom remarked to me in our last conversation, from 2009, when I asked why he thought more filmmakers didn't adopt his working methods: "I like the idea that when you start a film there's a certain amount of freedom, that the actors have a certain amount of freedom, that the camera can respond to what's happening in terms of the action rather than it all being preorganized. . . . And that's a choice you have to make. It depends on what type of cinema you like to make, what type of cinema you like to watch."

Following the customary guidelines for this series, the interviews have been arranged in chronological order but have not been edited from the form in which they originally appeared. The reader may therefore encounter repetitions in Winterbottom's responses, as well as the questions posed, despite the time range and different circumstances under which these conversations were conducted. Hopefully, these linguistic echoes will provide further evidence to scholars and film-curious readers that Winterbottom has remained consistent not only in his general attitude toward narrative cinema, but also the manner in which he articulates his thoughts and preoccupations to a variety of interlocutors when discussing his projects.

For agreeing quite charitably to my proposal for this book, I am deeply grateful to Leila Salisbury and Peter Brunette at the University Press of Mississippi, who have made this interview series an essential and indispensable resource for critics, filmmakers, academics, and general readers. Thanks to her editorial diligence, UPM staffer Valerie Jones was particularly helpful in guiding this book from the manuscript stage forward. I owe a sincere debt of gratitude as well to Leighton Walter and Catherine Chomat for their sterling translation of Ciment and Tobin's *Positif* interview, which appears here in English for the first time. They worked diligently with me on several iterations of the text, facing down the unenviable task of rendering a French-language interview originally conducted in English back into Winterbottom's native tongue. I assume full responsibility, however, for any errors, inconsistencies, or awkwardness in the final version.

I am further indebted to the staff at the New York Public Library for the Performing Arts and MoMA Queens, as well as Rob Winter and Geoff Andrew at the British Film Institute, for helping me gather research materials. Many people have contributed to this book in ways they may not be aware of. For support, advice, and encouragement, I am lucky to have a friend as sincere and wise as Eric Hynes, a critic for the ages. My illustrious colleagues at *Reverse Shot*, Michael Koresky and Jeff Reichert, have inspired me in innumerable ways too, not least through their own writings. This book would simply not exist, though, without Sabine Hrechdakian, whose devotion and unflagging patience throughout the entire process have been unearned, but deeply appreciated. Finally, special thanks to *Boston Globe* arts editor Scott Heller, who has written insightfully on Winterbottom himself, for first introducing me to his films.

DS

Chronology

1961   Born on March 29, 1961, in Blackburn, Lancashire, a working-class industrial town in northern England, son of Barrie, a production engineer for Phillips, and Jean (formerly Shaw), a primary-school teacher. Attends Queen Elizabeth's Grammar School.

1979   Attends Balliol College, Oxford University, reading in English, and meets Frank Cottrell Boyce, future screenwriter and a frequent collaborator. Joins a film club and discovers New German Cinema.

1983   Enrolls in post-graduate film and television courses at the University of Bristol and at the Polytechnic of Central London, while apprenticing in the editing rooms at Thames Television. Meets Andrew Eaton through mutual friend and fellow director Marc Evans.

1986   Meets long-term partner Sabrina Broadbent.

1988   Works for six months as a production assistant for Lindsay Anderson ("holding cups of tea," as he's often quipped) on a BBC documentary about British cinema.

1989   Spends six months in Sweden, trailing Ingmar Bergman and interviewing his frequent collaborators (Sven Nykvist, Liv Ullmann, Bibi Andersson, Max Von Sydow) for a pair of sixty-minute TV documentaries on the director. *Ingmar Bergman: The Director* and *Ingmar Bergman: The Magic Lantern* air on the BBC. Directs *True Romance*, a half-hour television program for children, and *Strangers*.

1990   Directs *Forget About Me*, a feature scripted by Frank Cottrell Boyce for Thames Television, and an episode of *Inspector Alleyn Mysteries*, "Death at the Bar," for the BBC.

1991   Completes another feature, *Under the Sun*, for Thames Television, among other projects. Winterbottom's eldest daughter is born.

1993   Directs a BBC feature, *Love Lies Bleeding*, and the inaugural episode of *Cracker*, "The Mad Woman in the Attic," edited by Trevor Waite. Among the cast are Christopher Eccleston and Kieran O'Brien, who would later star in two Winterbottom feature films.

1994   Approached by Andrew Eaton, now a BBC producer, Winterbottom directs the widely acclaimed four-part miniseries *Family*, based on a teleplay by author Roddy Doyle. Starts a production company, Revolution Films, with Eaton. Youngest daughter is born.

1995   *Butterfly Kiss* debuts in competition at the Berlin International Film Festival. *Variety* calls it "breathtakingly original." Winterbottom also picks up a nomination for Best Young Film at the European Film Awards. *Go Now*, the first Revolution Films production, debuts at the Edinburgh Film Festival in August, followed by a BBC premiere. Works on a screenplay about the war in Sarajevo.

1996   Finishes filming *Jude*, an adaptation of Thomas Hardy's classic novel starring Chris Eccleston and Kate Winslet, in January and travels to Sarajevo to scout locations. *Jude* is released in October. *Go Now* is nominated for a BAFTA award as Best Single TV Drama.

1997   Miramax Films releases *Welcome to Sarajevo*, which competes for the Palme d'Or in May at the Cannes Film Festival.

1998   *I Want You* enters the competition at the Berlinale in February. Shoots *With or Without You* in July and *Wonderland* in November. Revolution Films produces Marc Evans's *Resurrection Man*, with Winterbottom acting as executive producer.

1999   Debuts *Wonderland* at Cannes and wins a British Independent Film Award for Best British Film. *With or Without You* premieres at the Venice Film Festival.

2000   Begins filming the widescreen drama *Kingdom Come*, another Hardy adaptation relocated to the Gold Rush period in the American West, amid harsh conditions at Fortress Mountain in Alberta, Canada. For legal reasons, the title is changed to *The Claim* and released in December. Winterbottom reportedly leaves Sabrina Broadbent for Sarah Polley, who plays Hope in the film. The relationship is short-lived.

2001   In February, *The Claim* screens at the Berlin Film Festival. Shoots

24 Hour Party People, a cheeky drama about Factory Records honcho Tony Wilson and the Manchester music scene.

2002 *24 Hour Party People* lands in competition at Cannes and wins a British Independent Film Award for Best Achievement in Production. Acts as executive producer on Damien O'Donnell's *Heartlands.* Completes *The Silk Road* on location in Pakistan, Turkey, and Iran with a skeleton crew. The title is later changed to *In This World* when it debuts at the London Film Festival.

2003 Begins shooting *Code 46* in Shanghai, Dubai, and London. Wins the Golden Bear, the Peace Film Award, and the Prize of the Ecumenical Jury at the Berlin Film Festival for *In This World.* Shares executive-producer credit with Eaton on Stephen Fry's *Bright Young Things.* Commences post-production on *Code 46* in March. Premieres the film in September at the Venice Film Festival.

2004 Sabrina Broadbent, Winterbottom's former partner and the mother of his two daughters, publishes *Descent,* a critically acclaimed roman à clef about a woman's disastrous marriage to a high-strung filmmaker who's always elsewhere. *9 Songs* draws controversy at Cannes for its sexually explicit love scenes and is given an X rating in Australia. Winterbottom aggressively defends the film to the press. Begins production on *Tristram Shandy: A Cock and Bull Story* in October at Shandy Hall, Coxwold, and other locations in England.

2005 Has a falling-out with longtime writing partner Frank Cottrell Boyce, who removes his name from *A Cock and Bull Story.* Postproduction begins in January. Completes the film in July and is profiled by the *New York Times Magazine.* The same month, Winterbottom begins shooting *The Road to Guantánamo* with co-director Mat Whitecross in Pakistan, Iran, and Afghanistan. When *Shandy* officially debuts at the Toronto Film Festival in September, Boyce's contribution is credited to "Martin Hardy."

2006 Wins the Silver Bear at the Berlin Film Festival for *The Road to Guantánamo.* In the U.S., the MPAA bans the original promotional poster for the film, which references the Abu Ghraib torture photos. Flies to Namibia with Eaton to discuss adapting Mariane Pearl's memoir *A Mighty Heart* with Brad Pitt and Angelina Jolie. Puts another fully scripted, greenlighted project, *Genova,* on hold. Warner Bros. backs out of the production, but

Paramount Vantage steps up with financing. Shooting commences discreetly in August in Pakistan. A month later, the production is halted by local authorities, and the crew moves on to India. Jolie's presence in Mumbai ignites controversy.

2007   *A Mighty Heart* debuts at Cannes. In June, Winterbottom begins shooting *Genova* on location in Italy.

2008   Wins the top directing prize at the San Sebastián Film Festival for *Genova*. Begins working with co-director Mat Whitecross on a documentary adaptation of Naomi Klein's book *The Shock Doctrine*.

2009   *The Shock Doctrine* screens as a "work in progress" at the fifty-ninth Berlinale. Later that year, author Naomi Klein distances herself from the final edit of the film, which airs in Britain on More4. Wraps production in October on *The Killer Inside Me* in Guthrie, Oklahoma, the first feature Winterbottom has shot entirely in the United States.

2010   Unveils *The Killer Inside Me* at the Sundance Film Festival in Park City, Utah. *The Shock Doctrine* makes its North American premiere in a special Sundance presentation. Announces his latest project, *The Promised Land*, a drama set in Palestine at the end of World War II starring Colin Firth and Jim Sturgess.

Filmography

1989
INGMAR BERGMAN: THE DIRECTOR (TV documentary)
Thames Television
Producer: Alan Horrox
Director: **Michael Winterbottom**
Narrator: Lindsay Anderson
Interviewees: Sven Nykvist, Maj-Britt Nilsson, Liv Ullman, Bibi Andersson, Max Von Sydow, Gunnar Fischer, Ewa Frohling, Birger Malmsten, Katinka Farago, Sylvia Ingmarsson, Harriet Andersson, Lasse Bergstrom, Erland Josephson
60 minutes

INGMAR BERGMAN: THE MAGIC LANTERN (TV documentary)
Thames Television
Producer: Alan Horrox
Director: **Michael Winterbottom**
Editor: Dan Carter
60 minutes

DRAMARAMA: "ROSIE THE GREAT" (TV series, one episode)
Thames Television
Producer: Richard J. Staniforth
Director: **Michael Winterbottom**
Screenplay: David Stafford
Editor: Nigel Bell
Cast: Sarah Anson (Janis Hopkins), Peter Capaldi (British Ambassador), Susan Denaker (U.S. Ambassador), Conrad Evans (Reverend McNeil)

1990
FORGET ABOUT ME (TV feature)
Thames Television, Magyar Televizio Muvelodesi Foszerkesztoseg

(MTV)
Producer: Richard Handford
Director: **Michael Winterbottom**
Screenplay: Frank Cottrell Boyce
Photography: Ray Orton
Editor: Olivia Hetreed
Production Designer: Katalin Kalmár
Costume Designers: Philip Crichton, Eva Zalavari
Cast: Ewen Bremner (Broke), Brian McCardie (Bunny), Zsuzsanna Várkonyi (Czilla), Altay Lawrence (Sconehead), Attila Grandpierre (Attila), Katalin Pataki (Anna)
72 minutes

1991
SHRINKS (TV series, one episode)
Euston Films
Producer: Jackie Stoller
Director: **Michael Winterbottom**
Screenplay: Richard O'Keeffe, Jonathan Rich
Editors: Michael John Bateman, Graham Walker
Cast: Bill Paterson (Matt Hennessey), Yvonne Bryceland (Magda Myers), Patricia Kerrigan (Win Bargate), Brian Protheroe (Leo Brompton), Simon Jones (Jack Cavendish), David Thewlis (Terry Slater)

TIME RIDERS (TV series, four 25-minute episodes)
Thames Television
Producer: Alan Horrox
Director: **Michael Winterbottom**
Screenplay: Jim Eldridge
Editors: Olivia Hetreed, Geraldine Phillips
Music: Debbie Wiseman
Production Designer: Hayden Pearce
Cast: Haydn Gwynne (B. B. Miller), Clive Merrison (Professor Crow), Paul Bown (Captain), Brinley Jenkins (Judge), Ian McNeice (Leather Hardbones), James Saxon (Lord Chalmerston), Julie T. Wallace (Lady Chalmerston), Kenneth Hall (Ben Hardy), Kerry Swale (Hepworth), Gavin Richards (Witchfinder General)

BOON: "CAB RANK COWBOYS" (TV series, one episode)
ITV
Producer: Simon Lewis
Director: **Michael Winterbottom**
Screenplay: Peter Mann
Director of Photography: Don Perrin
Editor: John Hawkins
Sound: Paul Bennett, Peter Dyson
Cast: Michael Elphick (Ken Boon), Neil Morrissey (Rocky), David
Daker (Harry Crawford), Elizabeth Carling (Laura Marsh), Suzanna
Hamilton (Judy), Stratford Johns (John), Samantha Morton (Mandy),
Roger Lloyd-Pack (Ray Watts), Mark Moraghan (Wayne), James Boaden
(Gavin)
60 minutes

1992
UNDER THE SUN (TV feature)
Thames Television
Producer: Alan Horrox
Director: **Michael Winterbottom**
Story: **Michael Winterbottom** and Susan Campbell
Screenplay: Susan Campbell
Director of Photography: Daf Hobson
Costume Designer: Rachael Fleming
Sound: Aad Wirtz
Cast: Kate Hardie (Ellie), Stella Maris (Maria), Arturo Venegas (Felipe),
Caroline Catz (Linda)
77 minutes

1993
INSPECTOR ALLEYN MYSTERIES: "DEATH AT THE BAR" (TV series,
one episode)
BBC
Producer: George Gallaccio
Director: **Michael Winterbottom**
Screenplay: Alfred Shaughnessy
Director of Photography: John Walker
Editor: Jackie Powell, Robin Graham Scott
Production Designer: Martin Methven

Costume Designer: Ken Trew
Music: Ray Russell
Sound: Steve Fish, Douglas Mawson
Cast: Patrick Malahide (Chief Inspector Alleyn), William Simons (Inspector Fox), Kate Hardie (Decima Pomeroy), Alan Gilchrist (P.C. Oates), David Calder (Robert Legge), Alex Jennings (Sebastian Parish), Ben Daniels (Norman Cubitt), Anna Cropper (Violet Duffy), Peter Gale (Dr. Mordent)

LOVE LIES BLEEDING (TV feature)
BBC Northern Ireland
Producer: Robert Cooper
Director: **Michael Winterbottom**
Screenplay: Ronan Bennett
Cinematography: Eric Gillespie
Editor: David Spiers
Production Designer: Tom McCullagh
Sound: Aad Wirtz, Bryan Elliott
Cast: Mark Rylance (Conn), Elizabeth Bourgine (Sophie Allen), John Kavanagh (Sean Kerrigan), Brendan Gleeson (Thomas Macken), Tony Doyle (Geordie Wilson), Robert Patterson (Artie Flynn), George Shane (Gerry Ellis), James Nesbitt (Niall), Stuart Graham (Alex Mallie), Tim Loane (Robinson), Bosco Hogan (Rory McGinn), Margaret D'Arcy (Lily), Emma Jordan (Layla)
89 minutes

CRACKER: "THE MAD WOMAN IN THE ATTIC" (two-part TV series pilot)
ITV
Producer: Gub Neal
Director: **Michael Winterbottom**
Screenplay: Jimmy McGovern
Director of Photography: Ivan Strasburg
Editor: Trevor Waite
Assistant Editor: Peter Christelis
Production Designer: Chris Wilkinson
Costume Designer: Tudor George
Art Director: David Butterworth
Music: Julian Wastall

Cast: Robbie Coltrane (Dr Eddie "Fitz" Fitzgerald), Barbara Flynn (Judith Fitzgerald), Christopher Eccleston (DCI David Bilborough), Lorcan Cranitch (DS Jimmy Beck), Geraldine Somerville (DS Jane Penhaligon), Kieran O'Brien (Mark Fitzgerald), Adrian Dunbar (Thomas Kelly), Kika Markham (Ann Appleby), John Grillo (Simon Appleby)
100 minutes

1994
FAMILY (four-part TV miniseries)
BBC
Producer: Andrew Eaton
Director: **Michael Winterbottom**
Screenplay: Roddy Doyle
Director of Photography: Daf Hobson
Editor: Trevor Waite
Production Designer: Mark Geraghty
Art Director: Fiona Daly
Music: John Harle
Cast: Sean McGinley (Charlo Spencer), Ger Ryan (Paula Spencer), Barry Ward (John Paul Spencer), Des McAleer (Ray Harris), Gemma Butterly (Leanne Spencer), Neilí Conroy (Nicola Spencer), Jake Williams (Jack Spencer)
200 minutes

1995
BUTTERFLY KISS
British Screen Productions, Dan Films, Merseyside Film Production Fund
Producer: Julie Baines
Director: **Michael Winterbottom**
Screenplay: Frank Cottrell Boyce
Director of Photography: Seamus McGarvey
Editor: Trevor Waite
Production Designer: Rupert Miles
Costume Designer: Rachael Fleming
Music: John Harle
Sound: Ronald Bailey
Cast: Amanda Plummer (Eunice), Saskia Reeves (Miriam), Kathy Jamieson (Wendy), Des McAleer (Eric McDermott), Fine Time Fontayne

(Tony), Freda Dowie (Elsie), Ricky Tomlinson (Robert), Paul Bown (Gary), Emily Aston (Katie), Lisa Riley (Danielle), Paula Tilbrook (Ella), Joanne Cook (Angela), Katy Murphy (Judith)
35 mm, B&W and color, 88 minutes

CINEMA EUROPE: THE OTHER HOLLYWOOD: "ART'S PROMISED LAND" (TV mini-series episode)
Photoplay Productions
Producers: David Gill, Kevin Brownlow
Director: **Michael Winterbottom**
Music: Philip Appleby, Carl Davis, Nic Raine
Narrator: Kenneth Branagh
B&W and color, 60 minutes

GO NOW
Revolution Films, BBC
Producer: Andrew Eaton
Director: **Michael Winterbottom**
Screenplay: Jimmy McGovern, Paul Henry Powell
Director of Photography: Daf Hobson
Editor: Trevor Waite
Assistant Editor: Peter Christelis
Production Designer: Hayden Pearce
Art Designer: Frazer Pearce
Costume Designer: Rachael Fleming
Music: Alastair Gavin
Sound: Martin Trevis
Cast: Robert Carlyle (Nick Cameron), Juliet Aubrey (Karen), James Nesbitt (Tony), Sophie Okonedo (Paula), Tom Watson (Bill Cameron), Barbara Rafferty (Madge Cameron), Berwick Kaler (Sammy), Darren Tighe (Dell), Sean McKenzie (George), John Brobbey (Geoff), Sara Stockbridge (Bridget), Tony Curran (Chris Cameron), Erin McMahon (Julie Cameron), Sean Rocks (Charlie), Roger Ashton-Griffiths (Walsh), David Schneider (doctor), Susie Fugle (scan doctor)
81 minutes

1996
JUDE
Revolution Films, PolyGram Filmed Entertainment, BBC Films

Producer: Andrew Eaton
Director: **Michael Winterbottom**
Screenplay: Hossein Amini, based on the novel by Thomas Hardy
Director of Photography: Eduardo Serra
Editor: Trevor Waite
Production Designer: Joseph Bennett
Costume Designer: Janty Yates
Music: Adrian Johnston
Sound: Kant Pan, Martin Trevis
Cast: Christopher Eccleston (Jude Fawley), Kate Winslet (Sue Bridehead), Rachel Griffiths (Arabella), Liam Cunningham (Phillotson), June Whitfield (Aunt Drusilla), James Daley (Jude, as a boy), Ross Colvin Turnbull (little Jude), James Nesbitt (Uncle Joe), Paul Bown (Uncle Jim), Caitlin Bossley (Anny), Emma Turner (Sarah), Mark Lambert (Tinker Taylor), Amanda Ryan (gypsy saleswoman), Vernon Dobtcheff (curator), Freda Dowie (elderly landlady), Dexter Fletcher (priest), Ken Jones (Mr. Biles), Paul Copley (Mr. Willis)
35 mm, B&W and color, 123 minutes

1997
WELCOME TO SARAJEVO
Channel Four Films, Miramax Films, Dragon Pictures
Producer: Graham Broadbent, Damian Jones
Director: **Michael Winterbottom**
Screenplay: Frank Cottrell Boyce, based on *Natasha's Story* by Michael Nicholson
Director of Photography: Daf Hobson
Editor: Trevor Waite
Production Designer: Mark Geraghty
Costume Designer: Janty Yates
Music: Adrian Johnston
Sound: Martin Trevis
Cast: Stephen Dillane (Michael Henderson), Woody Harrelson (Flynn), Marisa Tomei (Nina), Emira Nusevic (Emira), Kerry Fox (Jane Carson), Goran Visnjic (Risto), James Nesbitt (Gregg), Emily Lloyd (Annie McGee), Juliet Aubrey (Helen Henderson), Igor Dzambazov (Jacket), Gordana Gadzic (Mrs. Savic), Drazen Sivak (Zeljko), Davor Janjic (Dragan), Vesna Orel (Munira), Vladimir Jokanovic (Emira's uncle)
Super 35, color, 103 minutes

1998
I WANT YOU
Revolution Films, PolyGram Filmed Entertainment
Producer: Andrew Eaton
Director: **Michael Winterbottom**
Screenplay: Eoin McNamee
Director of Photography: Slawomir Idziak
Editor: Trevor Waite
First Assistant Editor: Peter Christelis
Production Designer: Mark Tildesley
Costume Designer: Rachael Fleming
Art Directors: David Bowes, David Bryan
Music: Adrian Johnston
Sound: Martin Trevis
Cast: Rachel Weisz (Helen), Alessandro Nivola (Martin), Labina Mite-
vska (Smokey), Luka Petrusic (Honda), Carmen Ejogo (Amber), Graham
Crowden (old man), Ben Daniels (Bob), Geraldine O'Rawe (Sonja), Des
McAleer (florist), Steve John Shepherd (Sam), David Hounslow (Frank)
35 mm, color, 87 minutes

1999
WITH OR WITHOUT YOU
Revolution Films
Producer: Andrew Eaton
Director: **Michael Winterbottom**
Screenplay: John Forte
Director of Photography: Benoît Delhomme
Editor: Trevor Waite
Additional Editing: Peter Christelis
Production Designer: Mark Tildesley
Costume Designer: Janty Yates
Music Director: Adrian Johnston
Sound: Martin Trevis
Casting Director: Wendy Brazington
Cast: Christopher Eccleston (Vincent), Dervla Kirwan (Rosie), Yvan At-
tal (Benoit), Julie Graham (Cathy), Alun Armstrong (Sammy), Lloyd
Hutchinson (Neil), Michael Liebman (Brian), Doon MacKichan (Dei-
dre), Gordon Kennedy (Ormonde), Fionnula Flanagan (Irene), Dan
Gordon (Terry), Donna Dent (Lillian), Thomas Baker (Gary), Peter

Ballance (Andrew), Katia Caballero (Caroline)
Color, 93 minutes

WONDERLAND
Revolution Films, PolyGram Filmed Entertainment, Kismet Film Company, BBC Films, Universal Pictures
Producers: Andrew Eaton, Michele Camarda, Gina Carter
Director: **Michael Winterbottom**
Screenplay: Laurence Coriat
Director of Photography: Sean Bobbitt
Editor: Trevor Waite
Production Designer: Mark Tildesley
Costume Designer: Natalie Ward
Music: Michael Nyman
Sound: Richard Flynn
Casting Director: Wendy Brazington
Cast: Shirley Henderson (Debbie), Gina McKee (Nadia), Molly Parker (Molly), Ian Hart (Dan), John Simm (Eddie), Stuart Townsend (Tim), Kika Markham (Eileen), Jack Shepherd (Bill), Enzo Cilenti (Darren), Sarah-Jane Potts (Melanie), David Fahm (Franklyn), Ellen Thomas (Donna), Peter Marfleet (Jack), Nathan Constance (Alex), Anton Saunders (Danny)
16 mm, color, 108 minutes

2000
THE CLAIM
Revolution Films, Pathé Pictures, Arts Council of England, Canal+, BBC Films, Alliance Atlantis, Grosvenor Park, Alberta Foundation for the Arts, DB Entertainment
Producer: Andrew Eaton
Director: **Michael Winterbottom**
Screenplay: Frank Cottrell Boyce, partly based on Thomas Hardy's novel *The Mayor of Casterbridge*
Director of Photography: Alwin H. Kuchler
Editor: Trevor Waite
Production Designers: Mark Tildesley, Ken Rempel
Costume Designer: Joanne Hansen
Music: Michael Nyman
Sound: Howard Bargroff, Conor Mackey

Casting Directors: Wendy Brazington, Kerry Barden, Billy Hopkins, Suzanne Smith
Cast: Peter Mullan (Daniel Dillon), Milla Jovovich (Lucia), Wes Bentley (Dalglish), Nastassja Kinski (Elena Dillon), Sarah Polley (Hope), Sean McGinley (Mr. Sweetley), Shirley Henderson (Annie), Barry Ward (young Dillon), Karolina Muller (young Elena), Kate Hennig (Vauneen), Marie Brassard (French Sue), Duncan Fraser (Crocker), Julian Richings (Francis Bellanger)
35 mm, color, 120 minutes

2002
24 HOUR PARTY PEOPLE
Revolution Films, Film Consortium, FilmFour, UK Film Council, Channel Four, Baby Cow Productions
Producer: Andrew Eaton
Director: **Michael Winterbottom**
Screenplay: Frank Cottrell Boyce
Director of Photography: Robby Muller
Editor: Trevor Waite
Production Designer: Mark Tildesley
Costume Designer: Natalie Ward, Stephen Noble
Sound: Stuart Wilson, Aad Wirtz
Casting Director: Wendy Brazington
Cast: Steve Coogan (Tony Wilson), Lennie James (Alan Erasmus), Shirley Henderson (Lindsay Wilson), Paddy Considine (Rob Gretton), Andy Serkis (Martin Hannett), Sean Harris (Ian Curtis), John Simm (Bernard Sumner), Ralf Little (Peter Hook), Danny Cunningham (Shaun Ryder), Chris Coghill (Bez), Paul Popplewell (Paul Ryder), Keith Allen (Roger Ames), Rob Brydon (Ryan Letts), Mark Windows (Johnny Rotten), Enzo Cilenti (Peter Saville), Ron Cook (Derek Ryder), Dave Gorman (John the postman), Peter Kay (Don Tonay), Kate Magowan (Yvette Wilson), Kieran O'Brien (Nathan McGough), Simon Pegg (journalist), Rowetta (herself), Paul Ryder (Pel), John Thomson (Charles), Raymond Waring (Vini Reilly), Nick Clarke (Gaz), Toby Salaman (Sir Keith Joseph), Helen Schlesinger (Hilary), Christopher Eccleston (tramp), Peter Gunn (farmer), Howard Devoto (cleaner), Mark E. Smith (punter), Tony Wilson (studio director)
Digital video, 35 mm transfer, 117 minutes

IN THIS WORLD
Revolution Films, BBC Films, UK Film Council, Film Consortium
Producer: Andrew Eaton, Anita Overland
Director: **Michael Winterbottom**
Screenplay: Tony Grisoni
Director of Photography: Marcel Zyskind
Editor: Peter Christelis
Music: Dario Marianelli
Sound: Stuart Wilson
Casting Director: Wendy Brazington
Cast: Jamal Udin Torabi (Jamal), Enayatullah (Enayat), Imran Para-
cha (travel agent), Hiddayatullah (Enayat's brother), Jamau (Enayat's
father), Allah Bauhsh (Farid), Ahsan Raza (moneychanger), Mirwais
Torabi (Jamal's older brother), Amanullah Torabi (Jamal's younger
brother), Hossain Baghaeian (Behrooz), Yaaghoob Nosraj Poor (Kurdish
father), Ghodrat Poor (Kurdish mother), Kerem Atabeyoglu (police-
man), Erham Sekizcan (factory boss), Nabil Elouahabi (Yusif), Paul Popplewell (voice-over)
Digital video, 35 mm transfer, color, 88 minutes

2003
CODE 46
Revolution Films, BBC Films
Producer: Andrew Eaton
Director: **Michael Winterbottom**
Screenplay: Frank Cottrell Boyce
Directors of Photography: Alwin H. Kuchler, Marcel Zyskind
Editor: Peter Christelis
Production Designer: Mark Tildesley
Art Directors: Mark Digby, Denis Schnegg
Costume Designer: Natalie Ward
Casting Director: Wendy Brazington
Music: The Free Association
Sound: Stuart Wilson
Cast: Tim Robbins (William), Samantha Morton (Maria Gonzalez),
Jeanne Balibar (Sylvie), Natalie Mendoza (Sphinx receptionist), Es-
sie Davis (doctor), Om Puri (Bahkland), Emil Marwa (Mohan), Nabil
Elouahabi (vendor), David Fahm (Damian Alekan), Shelley King (Wil-
liam's boss), Nina Fog (Wole), Bruno Lastra (Bikku), Kerry Shale (clinic

doctor), Benedict Wong (medic), Mick Jones (himself)
Super 35, color, 93 minutes

2004
9 SONGS
Revolution Films
Producer: Andrew Eaton, **Michael Winterbottom**
Associate Producer: Melissa Parmenter
Director: **Michael Winterbottom**
Director of Photography: Marcel Zyskind
Editors: Mat Whitecross, **Michael Winterbottom**
Music: Melissa Parmenter, Black Rebel Motorcycle Club, The Von Bon-
dies, Michael Nyman, Franz Ferdinand, Primal Scream, The Dandy
Warhols, Goldfrapp, Super Furry Animals
Sound: Stuart Wilson
Cast: Kieran O'Brien (Matt), Margo Stilley (Lisa)
Digital video, 35 mm transfer, color, 69 minutes

2005
TRISTRAM SHANDY: A COCK AND BULL STORY
Revolution Films, BBC Films, Scion Films, Baby Cow Productions, EM
Media
Producer: Andrew Eaton
Co-Producers: Wendy Brazington, Anita Overland
Director: **Michael Winterbottom**
Screenplay: "Martin Hardy" (Frank Cottrell Boyce and **Michael Win-
terbottom**), from the novel by Laurence Sterne
Director of Photography: Marcel Zyskind
Editor: Peter Christelis
Production Designer: John Paul Kelly
Costume Designer: Charlotte Walter
Music: Edward Nogria, Michael Nyman
Sound: Stuart Wilson
Casting Director: Wendy Brazington
Cast: Steve Coogan (Steve Coogan/Walter Shandy/Tristram Shandy),
Rob Brydon (Rob Brydon/Uncle Toby), Keeley Hawes (Elizabeth
Shandy), Shirley Henderson (Susannah/Shirley Henderson), Dylan
Moran (Dr Slop), David Walliams (parson), Jeremy Northam (Mark,
the director), Gillian Anderson (Widow Wadman/Gillian Anderson),

Benedict Wong (Ed), Naomie Harris (Jennie), Kelly Macdonald (Jenny), Elizabeth Berrington (Debbie), Mark Williams (Ingoldsby), Kieran O'Brien (Gary), Roger Allam (Adrian), James Fleet (Simon), Ian Hart (Joe), Ronni Ancona (Anita), Greg Wise (Greg), Stephen Fry (Patrick/ Parson Yorick), Raymond Waring (Corporal Trim), Paul Kynman (Obadiah), Mark Tandy (London doctor), Jack Shepherd (surgeon), Stephen Rodrick (reporter), Stuart Wilson (sound mixer), Tony Wilson (TV interviewer)
Digital video, 35 mm transfer, 94 minutes

2006
THE ROAD TO GUANTÁNAMO
Revolution Films, Screen West Midlands, FilmFour
Producers: Andrew Eaton, Melissa Parmenter
Directors: **Michael Winterbottom**, Mat Whitecross
Director of Photography: Marcel Zyskind
Editors: **Michael Winterbottom**, Mat Whitecross
Production Designer: Mark Digby
Music: Harry Escott, Molly Nyman
Sound: Stuart Wilson
Casting Director: Wendy Brazington
Cast: Riz Ahmed (Shafiq), Farhad Harun (Ruhel), Arfan Usman (Asif), Waqar Siddiqui (Monir), Shahid Iqbal (Zahid), Jason Salkey, Jacob Gaffney, Mark Holden (US interrogators in Pakistan), Adam James (SAS interrogator), Brian Flaherty, Steven Beckingham (Camp X-ray guard), Mark Sproston (embassy man), Sara Stewart (Washington woman), Sasha Pick (CIA interrogator), Kieran O'Brien (voiceover)
Digital video, 35 mm transfer, color, 95 minutes

2007
A MIGHTY HEART
Revolution Films, Paramount Vantage, Plan B Entertainment
Producers: Andrew Eaton, Dede Gardner, Brad Pitt
Co-Producer: Anita Overland
Director: **Michael Winterbottom**
Screenplay: John Orloff, from Mariane Pearl and Sarah Crichton's memoir, *A Mighty Heart: The Brave Life and Death of My Husband, Danny Pearl*
Director of Photography: Marcel Zyskind

Editor: Peter Christelis
Production Designer: Mark Digby
Costume Designer: Charlotte Walter
Music: Harry Escott, Molly Nyman
Sound: Stuart Wilson, Rashad Omar
Casting Directors: Wendy Brazington, Ellen Lewis
Cast: Angelina Jolie (Mariane Pearl), Dan Futterman (Danny Pearl), Will Patton (Randall Bennett), Archie Panjabi (Asra), Irfan Khan (Captain), Mohammed Afzal (Shabbir), Azfar Ali (Azfar), Denis O'Hare (John Bussey), Zachary Coffin (Matt McDowell), Demetri Goritsas (John Skelton), Jillian Armenante (Maureen Platt), Sajid Hasan (Zafir), Gary Wilmes (Steve Levine)
Digital video, 35 mm, color, 100 minutes

2008
GENOVA
Revolution Films, FilmFour, Aramid Entertainment Fund
Producer: Andrew Eaton, **Michael Winterbottom**
Co-Producer: Wendy Brazington
Director: **Michael Winterbottom**
Screenplay: Laurence Coriat, **Michael Winterbottom**
Director of Photography: Marcel Zyskind
Editor: Paul Monaghan
Production Designer: Mark Digby
Costume Designer: Celia Yau
Music: Melissa Parmenter
Sound: Stuart Wilson
Casting Director: Wendy Brazington
Cast: Colin Firth (Joe), Catherine Keener (Barbara), Willa Holland (Kelly), Perla Janey-Hardine (Mary), Hope Davis (Marianne), Demetri Goritsas (Steve), Kyle Griffin (Scott), Kerry Shale (Stephen), Sara Stewart (Susanna), Trevor White (Michael), Gary Wilmes (Dan), Alessandro Giuggioli (Lorenzo), Dante Ciari (Fabio), Gherardo Crucitti (Mauro)
Digital video, 35 mm transfer, color, 94 minutes

2009
THE SHOCK DOCTRINE
Revolution Films, Renegade Pictures
Producer: Andrew Eaton

Co-Producer: Melissa Parmenter
Directors: **Michael Winterbottom**, Mat Whitecross
Screenplay: Based on Naomi Klein's book *The Shock Doctrine: The Rise of Disaster Capitalism*
Editors: Paul Monaghan, Mat Whitecross, **Michael Winterbottom**
Sound: James Dandridge, Naomi Dandridge
Cast: Naomi Klein (herself), Kieran O'Brien (narrator)
Digital video, color, 79 minutes

2010
THE KILLER INSIDE ME
Revolution Films, Hero Entertainment, Indion Entertainment Group
Producer: Andrew Eaton, Bradford L. Schlei
Directors: **Michael Winterbottom**
Screenplay: John Curran and **Michael Winterbottom**, based on Jim Thompson's novel
Director of Photography: Marcel Zyskind
Editor: Mags Arnold
Production Designer: Mark Tildesley
Music: Melissa Parmenter
Sound: David O. Daniel
Cast: Casey Affleck (Lou Ford), Jessica Alba (Joyce Lakeland), Kate Hudson (Amy Stanton), Tom Bower (Sheriff Tom Maples), Jay R. Ferguson (Elmer Conway), Liam Aiken (Johnnie Pappas), Brent Briscoe (Bum/The Stranger), Ned Beatty, Elias Koteas, Bill Pullman
35 mm, color, 148 minutes

2007–present
SEVEN DAYS (TV project, still in production)
Revolution Films, Channel 4
Producer: Andrew Eaton
Director: **Michael Winterbottom**
Screenplay: Laurence Coriat, **Michael Winterbottom**
Sound: Adrian Bell, Paul Cameron
Cast: John Simm, Shirley Henderson, George Katt, Johnny Lynch, Laurence Richardson

Michael Winterbottom: Interviews

Wings of Desire

Geoff Andrew/1995

From *Time Out* (London), no. 1304 (16 August 1995). Reprinted by permission.

A busy man, Michael Winterbottom. Having already attracted attention for TV work like *Love Lies Bleeding*, the Roddy Doyle series *Family*, and the opening episode of *Cracker* he went on to make his first, low-budget (£400,000) theatrical feature, *Butterfly Kiss*, before following that with the BBC film *Go Now* (which premieres at the Edinburgh festival) and, currently in pre-production, a TV movie of *Jude the Obscure*. Right now, however, it's *Butterfly Kiss* that's of interest: an edgy, discomforting tale of two none-too-bright young girls on a murder spree in north-east England.

Winterbottom made the film—which stars Amanda Plummer as volatile psychopath Eunice and Saskia Reeves as Miriam, a naive homebody whose admiration for her new-found mentor impels her to indulge, even to become an accomplice to Eunice's murderous deeds—in close collaboration with screenwriter Frank Cottrell Boyce, with whom he had previously worked on the TV dramas *The Strangers* and *Forget About Me*. The inspiration for the story was twofold: "The true story of a guy who'd killed his baby boy—his wife had forgiven him but he couldn't forgive himself—and Frank wanting to do something about an abusive relationship where, from the outside, you can't understand why one person stays with the other but for some reason they just can't leave. Our interest was in the relationship between Miriam and Eunice—we didn't want it to be a psychological study of a murderer—and the killings actually came quite late into the story, as a series of tests for Miriam's belief that there's good in everyone. So it was the consequences of, rather than the reasons for, Eunice's actions that concerned us."

As seems inevitable these days in films about serial killers, *Butterfly Kiss* adopts a pretty non-judgmental attitude to Eunice and Miriam's exploits, even going so far in its depiction of their male victims as to echo Miriam's dismissal of one of them as "a pervert . . . who deserved to die." Did Winterbottom feel the movie expresses a moral point of view? "It has no particular moral as such, but it is a moral film. Clearly, Eunice does feel she's evil and needs to be punished, while Miriam runs around saying, 'Look, I love you; if love can redeem sin, I am that person.' But Eunice can't see that. So it's a perverse love story.

"Of course, what Eunice does is terrible, and that's acknowledged in the film; but one thing we didn't want was to have Eunice make a big speech whereby you'd realize she's actually a nice person but something had happened to her. We simply wanted to show Miriam proving her love. And it's that love, hopefully, which will make audiences stay with these characters, who basically make the film quite hard to watch."

That Winterbottom and Boyce were keen to offer something rather more complex than your run-of-the-mill serial-killer saga may be gleaned from the fact that its two leads start calling each other "Eu" (you) and "Mi" (me), which ties in with Miriam's assertion that her friend merely acts out the desires the rest of us dream of perpetrating: Eunice as the emergent id to Miriam's repressed ego. "One thing that attracted us," concedes Winterbottom, "was to take two opposites, neither of which is complete: Eunice is aggressive, experienced, Miriam does nothing at all. So that's certainly one possible idea. But it's not as if we wanted the film to be read in one particular way."

Likewise, on the conceit of producing a British variation on an essentially American genre: "We liked the idea of a British road movie, which is so anachronistic it's a terrible idea. In Britain, you don't have that same sense of a journey, of freedom, as you do in America. But *Butterfly Kiss* is about people going round and round, not going anywhere; everywhere looks the same, clogged with traffic. Miriam and Eunice don't even have cars—half the time they're *walking* along the side of the road! At the same time, it's also a movie specifically set in the north-east, but we wanted to get away from those images of red-brick towns and beautiful dales. It's the anonymity of the place that matters here."

Winterbottom The (Increasingly Less) Obscure

Jan Stuart/1996

Film buffs who mourn the heyday of the great European directors—the Fellinis, the Truffauts, the Bergmans—are beginning to shift their gaze away from the continent. More and more, nervy, trailblazing movies are emerging from the long-dormant British Isles. This year alone, Mike Leigh (*Secrets & Lies*), Danny Boyle (*Trainspotting*), Hettie MacDonald (*Beautiful Thing*) and, this December, Terry George (*Some Mother's Son*) are juicing up the scene with pictures that manage to be at once emotionally jolting, cinematically fresh, and uncommonly user-friendly to American audiences.

Auteur watchers may have a little more trouble getting a handle on Michael Winterbottom. This is not to say that *Jude*, his loving adaptation of Thomas Hardy's classic novel *Jude the Obscure* opening this Friday, is a difficult study. What is elusive is a signature style, or field of interest. Painterly, somber, and period in setting, his second film would seem to bear little relation to his first, a mordant portrait of a lesbian serial killer called *Butterfly Kiss*, or his next, *Sarajevo*, a big-budget epic on the recent Bosnian war.

Winterbottom's *Jude* may draw its biggest support not from cinephiles, however, but bibliophiles. Faithful without being slavish, immediate without stooping to anachronism, *Jude* is manna for lovers of literature-on-film still in toxic shock from warbling Quasimodos and lap-dancing Hester Prynnes.

Boyish and decidedly nonacademic-looking in black sneakers and

5

checkered pants, the thirty-five-year old Winterbottom suggests something more Tompkins Square slacker than Oxbridge literary society. Even though he already has his own production company with the disarmingly anarchic moniker of Revolution Films, the director is still a bit green on the movie-promo circuit. To wit, the first seven minutes of his interview are spent searching for the minibar in the sprawling hotel suite that Gramercy Pictures has bankrolled for him. (There is none.)

The serious-seeming Winterbottom, who holds a degree in English from Oxford, first read *Jude the Obscure* when he was fifteen. At the time, he was captivated by the love story at the heart of this late nineteenth-century saga of Jude Fawley (played by *Shallow Grave*'s Christopher Eccleston), a poor rural lad whose aspirations toward scholarly pursuits and the ministry are defeated by class limitations, social taboos, and libido. Specifically, he is tricked into marriage by Arabella (Rachel Griffiths) and bewitched by Sue Bridehead (*Sense and Sensibility*'s Kate Winslet), the free-thinking cousin of Jude who helps lead him off the straight and narrow path into a common-law relationship. "She was an ideal to me," recalls Winterbottom a little bashfully of that first reading. "I wondered why all women couldn't be like Sue Bridehead."

There are many, however, who may wonder at the whole point of Jude and Sue's obstacle-strewn life together. When Hardy wrote *Jude the Obscure* in 1895, he intended it in part as a double-pronged attack on a class system that prevented people from educating themselves out of indigence and on societal constraints that subjugated women and kept a lock on miserable marriages. With the proliferation of university scholarships and liberal divorce laws in the ensuing century, a movie of *Jude the Obscure* in 1996 may beg the question "Why now?" Winterbottom is nonplussed by the challenge of relevancy. "Here is someone who wants to change his life . . . There are many who want to improve their lives but can't for whatever reason: prejudice, economic problems. The same with marriage . . . The nature of the prejudice may have changed, but the ostracism is often exactly the same. So it's not a question of it being particularly relevant now, but always relevant."

Winterbottom, who disdains the Merchant-Ivory school of voluptuous visuals as "massage by film," chose a grittier, dust-kicking approach more akin to *Persuasion*, Roger Michell's recent take on Jane Austen. "Hardy isn't interested in costumes or colors of wallpaper or conventions of polite manners as some period novels. With *Jude*, the characters are interested in ideas, in poetry and literature, in 'Does God exist?' I think it would be a travesty to Hardy to make a film that seemed more interested in fripperies and details."

If there is any personal identification for Winterbottom in Hardy's tale, it is in a line where Jude confesses, "I tried to do in one generation what it takes two or three generations to do." Raised in a lower middle-class household in Blackburn, near Manchester, Winterbottom had a very strong sense of "each generation making a little more progress than the last."

When he and his brother earned the family's first university degrees, it clinched an upward path from his grandparents' grade-school education and factory work to his father's electronics career and mother's schoolteaching. "My generation doesn't have the same sense of confidence for their children," he says with characteristic earnestness. "I don't think people have quite the same optimism that they did in the sixties and seventies."

Optimism was in short supply in *Butterfly Kiss*, Winterbottom's acclaimed debut feature, a grunged-down *Thelma and Louise* that starred Amanda Plummer as a body-pierced drifter who goes on a killing tear with her adoring girlfriend. The script was initially far more sedate, but went increasingly over the top as Winterbottom encountered obstacles in getting it financed, a process that took more than two years. It may not be the first movie that transmutes the off-camera rigors of independent filmmaking into onscreen psychosis, but it may be the creepiest.

Jude, with its literary pedigree, was a relatively easy sell. For *Sarajevo*, his recently wrapped epic starring Woody Harrelson and Marisa Tomei, Winterbottom was recruited by Miramax and Channel Four Films. Based on true events, the film approaches the tragedy of Bosnia through a *Killing Fields* lens: from the vantage point of the journalists covering a nation under siege.

"Almost all of the journalists I talked to said the same thing: that there was something about that particular war that affected them more than any other conflict they reported on. In England, several newspapers and lots of journalists were actively campaigning for something to happen—Why aren't we sending in the troops? How can we allow this to go on?—rather than writing cool accounts of what was occurring."

Winterbottom encountered degrees of quiet heroism from the local crew in Sarajevo, where the filmmakers spent two weeks. "When we filmed a mortar attack that killed twenty-odd people in the street when they were queuing for bread [in 1992], the cameraman who was doing all the news-camera filming for us had been the news cameraman on the day it actually happened and saw all the bleeding people running through the street. And I thought, oh, my God, how is he going to cope with this? But he was keen on doing the film and getting all the details right.

"What interested me was the different ways people have of coping. Even when nothing was actually happening, you still couldn't go on with your lives, because this could be the day you'd go down the street and somebody would take a shot at you. A lot of people said that if the fighting started up again, they would just get out. Psychologically, they couldn't go back to the thought of trying to resist again."

Winterbottom and Andrew Eaton, his co-producer at Revolution Films, are hatching another Thomas Hardy–inspired project, a Gold Rush western spin-off of *The Mayor of Casterbridge*. "We originally sold the idea as a potato western. Everybody in his town was going to be Irish. But now it's going to be a European western, in which the population is all immigrants."

By the time Michael Winterbottom returns for an interview tour to hype *Sarajevo*, he should rate a hotel suite with a minibar. As he builds a portfolio of sober and weighty films, though, he flirts with the prospect of becoming the Ingmar Bergman of England.

When the possibility is suggested, he smiles, shrugs and responds, "Nothing wrong with being Ingmar Bergman. He managed to make fifty films before anyone stopped him."

People Who Are Excluded from Society: Interview with Michael Winterbottom

Michel Ciment and Yann Tobin/1996

From *Positif*, no. 430 (December 1996): 23–28. Reprinted by permission. Translated from French by Leighton Walter and Catherine Chomat.

Q: What is your background?

A: My family is from Lancashire, where my mother was a teacher and my father worked at Philips. We lived in a big housing complex next to a small town. The television was always on; this was how I discovered not only old films, but also the young English directors of the seventies, like Ken Loach and Mike Leigh. Later, I was a regular at local cinema clubs.

Q: Was the choice of the Northern English countryside in *Butterfly Kiss* and *Jude* connected to your upbringing there?

A: Yes, and that of Frank Cottrell Boyce, the screenwriter of *Butterfly Kiss*, who's from Liverpool. It was our first feature film, and to better our odds [we chose] to shoot this unusual story in familiar places.

Q: You started out by studying literature at Oxford. Were you already thinking about a career in film?

A: Not yet. I was simply someone who liked movies. It was at the university cinema club that the idea germinated. After Oxford I was in Bristol, where I took film courses. I was then hired as an assistant editor for television movies. Then Lindsay Anderson did a documentary on British cinema for which I was documentarian. After this, I made several small films for television and two documentaries on Ingmar Bergman.

Q: Were they personal projects?

A: With my producer I proposed them to Channel Four. I was lucky because of circumstances. In fact, it was especially during the preparation, when I immersed myself in his films over six months, that I really became passionate, not only for Bergman's oeuvre, in its immensity and diversity, but especially for his way of working, of controlling everything.

Q: Have you met him?

A: We did not film him, but he gave us several early films he had shot, and he recorded a little voice-over. He had the right to look at the editing, and we showed him the film for approval. There were two hour-long films, shot around his sixtieth birthday celebration in 1988: One, *Magic Lantern*, based on his personal films, was interwoven with extracts from his *Mémoires* in voiceover, and the other based on interviews with his collaborators.

Q: Was there a cinematographic school or trend that particularly influenced you?

A: The new German cinema during my years in the cinema club: Fassbinder, Wenders. In shooting *Butterfly Kiss*, I thought of their way of filming places that weren't cinematographic in and of themselves, of their sense of the atmosphere of a place.

Q: What was your first experience with fiction?

A: It was a half-hour television program for children, written by Frank Cottrell Boyce, titled *True Romance*—a little boy dreams of a love story with the neighbors' daughter, but she's too old for him. We continued with another film for children, *Strangers* [1989], and *Forget About Me* [1990], my first television feature film, which was shown at several festivals—a love story. Then *Under the Sun* [1992], with Kate Hardie, about a nineteen-year-old girl who decides to travel around the world, but doesn't get any further than Spain.

Q: How much freedom did you have in the choice of subjects?

A: A lot of freedom. I was very lucky. I have to say that the budgets were small, but were sufficient for shooting under the right conditions. The screenplay of *Under the Sun* was rewritten as filming progressed in Spain. The actors were young and not particularly experienced—like me! We could allow ourselves to make mistakes without suffering any consequences. *Love Lies Bleeding* [1992] was an autobiographical story by Ronan Bennett, about a prisoner out on a day leave, his connections with the Irish Republican Army, which he's part of, and with his girlfriend. Jimmy McGovern was the author of *Cracker*, a series for which I did the first episode, "The Madwoman in the Attic" [1993], with Chris Eccleston in the role of a criminologist who plays the detectives—an enormous success in England.

Q: Like many British filmmakers, you know how to move from one topic to the next, adapting your style.

A: Is that a good thing? The filmmakers people like, you recognize instantly, in every shot. This perhaps comes from the fact that with television, which forms most of us, directors rarely have a choice of subjects: they do film after film proposed by others. Screenwriters have more freedom, and one recognizes their films more easily. At the BBC, they start by buying a screenplay, then they call in a director to shoot it for them. If, from the beginning, it was me who chose my subjects and my screenwriters, it's because my TV producer, Allan Horrox, was in fact the director of the department and he let me do what I wanted.

Q: Was the series *Family,* adapted from a novel by Roddy Doyle, like those in his famous trilogy [*The Commitments, The Snapper, The Van*]?

A: No, it was the other way around: *Family* was written for television. Andrew Eaton, the producer, asked Roddy for an idea for a series and he proposed *Family.* During the production of the series, he began writing a novel inspired by the same characters, but enriched their stories, starting with the youth of the father and the mother.

Q: What was the format of the series?

A: Four one-hour episodes. But they are really four different films. Each one centered on a different member of the family: the father, the mother, the son, and the daughter. It was interesting to find, for each weekly episode, a specific style that corresponded to the point of view of the protagonist.

Q: So how did the choice of subject for *Butterfly Kiss* come about?

A: Frank Cottrell Boyce and I had collaborated on several television projects before we said to ourselves: "Let's write a movie screenplay." We came up with a project titled *Delirious,* about three twenty-year-old youths. The end was similar to that of *Butterfly Kiss:* someone sacrifices himself for someone else in Morecambe Bay. The people from British Screen were interested and encouraged us. We tried desperately to get the project going for two years, but in vain. Then we said to ourselves: "We could spend our whole life on *Delirious.* Let's write another one really quickly and shoot it, no matter what happens!" It was absolutely necessary that the film could be made cheaply—that was a condition of writing it. But it also had to be personal enough to justify this urgency. *Butterfly Kiss* cost around £400,000, with a crew of around twenty people.

Q: Who had the initial idea?

A: I was intrigued by a news item that I had read, an interview of a man who had done twenty years in prison for having killed his child. He had been out for five years and his former wife wanted them to get married again—he had forced her to divorce him when he was in jail. But he refused to reintegrate socially: Even though his wife and their eighteen-year-old daughter had forgiven him, he felt he was unpardonable. He didn't know what to do with his life and was living like a vagabond. As for Frank, he had his own ideas. By getting together and talking, we came up with a totally different story, that of *Butterfly Kiss*. Then, working from a fifteen-page treatment, he wrote the screenplay on his own. Frank is a very religious person: the mystical elements of the film are from him. He was inspired by two women he knew and created one character based on my point of departure. As for me, I had [an unrealized] project to do a documentary on people who practice piercing. Bit by bit, various elements were added, sometimes in a strange way— Frank's very stylized writing, with its stressed dialogue, was too disconnected from such a naturalistic environment.

Q: Were you aware from the start of the strange, unnerving aspect of *Butterfly Kiss*?

A: We knew that the two characters would be difficult to accept: Emotionally, the film wasn't easy, with these themes of redemption, of pardon and punishment. Eunice is a character who carries all her repression inside herself and lets it explode toward others. Jude is the opposite, a victim of outside events that he turns against himself. Eunice isn't a pleasant character, and Miriam [Saskia Reeves], for her part, is so limited. We thought that some people would hate the film! Everything was built on the final scene; it's the warmest of the film. We started with this moment of tenderness and then developed all the horror that preceded it.

Q: Have you felt the direct influence of typical American film genres, like serial-killer movies, film noir, or the road movie?

A: We told ourselves that shooting an English road movie seemed like the perfect recipe for a catastrophe. In addition, they don't have a car, and Eunice never stops saying she's turning in circles, that she keeps going by the same places. A road movie without a trip, that takes place in one location—that's the disconnect that attracted us. But it was more like a road movie that came to us via Wenders's Germany.

Q: Was the screenplay completely written before you started searching for locations?

A: Yes, but we had always known where the end of the film would be shot, in Morecambe Bay. In fact, because Frank and I knew the region well, it was less a matter of searching for locations than persuading people to let us film where we wanted. No one wanted us to shoot in gas stations. We were obliged to travel long distances.

Q: How did you choose the two actors?

A: I was familiar with Saskia's work. It wasn't an obvious choice. I was very attached to the solitary, closed side of this character in her pitiful service station. And in front of me there was this splendid creature, blond and full of life, the exact opposite of the homely and ungrateful girl I saw in my mind. But she was enthusiastic about the story. She had to get this awful hairdo, makeup, costumes. At the beginning of the project, I had thought of using two total unknowns, even nonprofessionals, so that people would constantly ask themselves, "Is this a documentary?" "Are they playing themselves?" But the screenplay was so stylized that two nonprofessionals could never have done it justice. No English actress who auditioned had the internal energy necessary for the role—they "acted" too much. I had seen Amanda in two films. Even though in real life she was nothing like the character, she possessed this bluntness, this energy that made you believe in her. The conditions of the shoot were very difficult for the actresses: limited means, very rudimentary comforts, and with the ceaseless noise of the highways, the filth. For weeks they were immersed in this world, and constantly had to concentrate.

Q: They complement each other beautifully.

A: Their relationship worked very well right from the start. They were diametrically opposed in their habits. Amanda wanted to try different, unexpected things, with each take. "Forget what we just did. Let's try something else." Saskia is much more controlled, working with each successive take to perfect the approach she'd chosen. A fascinating contrast.

Q: Did the shots of Miriam talking to the camera come from your idea of interviewing the killer?

A: We first planned on a voiceover. It was the character of Miriam who was remembering the story. Once the shoot was over, the voice recording session gave us the idea of writing these new scenes. Saskia took part, because she knew exactly what she was supposed to evoke. And this completely changed the editing. Without these scenes, Saskia was practically invisible compared to Eunice. With these back-and-forths, her character took on a much more interesting dimension.

Q: The image oscillates between realism and stylization, as does the entire film.

A: It was in starting to shoot the film that we agreed on the visual approach. I didn't want the film to seem like a documentary. Yet it was tempting: Seamus McGarvey, the cameraman, had a superb book of photos, very well known, on the [English] A1 highway, showing the most fascinating places, the most striking spots on the route. When I showed him the desolate shooting locations, oh my god! But this prompted him to systematically attempt to make each scene interesting. On the other hand, I loved this tension between the everyday places that everyone can immediately recognize, and this strange story.

Q: When did you create your production company, Revolution Films?

A: It was just after *Family*, my first collaboration with Andrew Eaton. We wanted the possibility of developing projects without having to go to other partners to finance the writing. We started with *Jude* and in between, I did *Go Now*.

Q: So after your first theatrical film, *Butterfly Kiss*, you went back to television with *Go Now*?

A: It was partly for financial reasons. I had worked six months on *Butterfly Kiss* practically without being paid, and I was happy to go back to television. Andrew and I started to look for a project for the BBC. Jimmy McGovern offered us a first look at this story he had written with Paul Henry Powell. It was about fifty minutes long. I liked it a lot and wanted to work with Jimmy again. He had met Paul in a writing workshop for multiple sclerosis patients. Things went really quickly: We decided to do it in November 1995, the BBC approved the screenplay in January 1996, and fifteen weeks later, the film was done.

Q: Would you have shot *Go Now* differently for the big screen?

A: A little, I think. I wasn't certain about the theatrical release. When we shot *Family*, we blew it up to 35mm and we made a version shortened by two hours for the festivals. Lots of people wanted to buy the distribution rights, and Roddy Doyle had refused. It was frustrating at the time, because I wanted it to be shown in theaters.

Q: But the style of *Go Now* isn't fundamentally different from certain films by Loach, for example, shot directly for the big screen.

A: It's a delicate question. I would be tempted, in one way, to say that there isn't a fundamental distinction, especially in Great Britain, where practically all films are co-produced by a television network. On the other hand, a number of made-for-television films end up being shown in theaters. The organization of the shooting isn't fundamentally different. But I remember being anxious at the time of *Butterfly Kiss*, when I would say to myself: "This is my first feature film." I think that it's more a question of subject than form. Whether one makes a movie for the small or big screen, you try to do so in a way that's as interesting as possible. But if someone had proposed the subject of *Go Now* for theaters, I don't know if I would have chosen it right away.

Q: The film is short, but one gets the feeling that it could have continued. You end it on a note of hope that's intentionally abrupt.

A: It was Paul's autobiographical narrative, and we all knew it: It gives the film its force, but also limits it in a way. Paul had been diagnosed years before, and had been quite handicapped for some time. At the time of the film, he was in remission and had just had a child: his life was then in an optimistic phase, and that's what he wanted to show through the film. That's why, undoubtedly, the film shies away from certain psychological aspects linked to the illness, in particular those pertaining to its totally unpredictable nature. At the same time, that's what makes it interesting: The film isn't content to talk about the illness; it also shows us a person like so many others, with his problems.

Q: The back-and-forth between comedy and pathos works very well.

A: We wanted to avoid the sentimental approach, the easiest one. We tried to make it sharper, harder . . . and funnier. Because it was Paul's personal story, there were delicate moments: for example, is it necessary that his girlfriend betray him? The BBC was very opposed to this, feeling that this made the character terribly unpleasant. And Paul told us: "My wife's going to have it out with me!"

Q: Why did you shoot the film in Bristol?

A: In the beginning the action took place in London, but I didn't want to shoot the film there. I knew this particular neighborhood of Bristol well, having lived there. It's easier to shoot in a place one knows. The place has an unusual atmosphere for an English town, with a very interesting social mix, lots of different communities living together. It's a little like Montpellier, or Lyon in Tavernier's *L'Horloger de Saint-Paul*. People come from everywhere to settle in this neighborhood, where there's also lots of old artisans.

Q: The cast brought together the stars of *Go Now* and *Jude*.

A: We worked on *Jude* during the shooting of *Go Now*. We thought that this would be kind of a trial run, to set the action in the world of building and construction.

Q: Robert Carlyle is remarkably believable in *Go Now*.

A: Because it was Paul's story, the medical resemblance didn't pose any problems. Robert was hired right before the shoot. He spent several days with Paul and, in Bristol, he met with a patients' association.

Q: *Jude* and *Go Now* have in common an everyday protagonist around whom an extraordinary drama unfolds.

A: There are also common points between *Jude* and *Butterfly Kiss*, which are like two faces of the same coin. I identified strongly with the central character in *Jude* from the moment I read the novel, and I hope that the public will also. Whereas in *Butterfly Kiss*, it's the other way around: I would like people to look at the characters first from outside, that they discover their world before entering into it, without immediately projecting themselves into it. In this sense, *Jude* is a more easily accessible film: You know right away which side to take.

Q: *Jude* is a project that you were entertaining for a long time.

A: Yes, but before *Family* we never seriously considered it. And suddenly, things went pretty quickly. Mark Shivas commissioned the screenplay. The moment it was ready, PolyGram immediately said yes. The fact that this was the adaptation of a classic very likely made things easier. *Jude the Obscure* was my favorite book. I must have read it four or five times during my adolescence. At the time I was living in the countryside, and Hardy, himself a provincial, projected himself a lot in Jude. This idealist, anti-conformist aspect, and this feeling of marginality gave the novel its power and its passion. Even though in life he succeeded at everything Jude dreamed of and failed at, [Hardy] always considered himself excluded from the intellectual elite of the time. Ironically, this book caused a scandal and was his last.

Q: Did you choose Hossein Amini yourself?

A: Yes. He was a very young author and we'd seen one of his films without knowing him personally. I had prepared a sort of summary of the book for him that already made certain choices. The book is thick but contains, like the film, an episodic, elliptical structure, very original for its time. For example, you learn at one point that he has two children and yet will never know their names.

Q: Did you prepare the film in detail with the director of photography?

A: There were several historical references, documents, black-and-white photos. But we had mostly discussed the overall construction of the film, and the mood that each part should evoke. We talked more about content than form. From that we worked out the visual aspects, eventually with the help of documents to be sure we were talking about the same thing. As for the camera movements, I have trouble making a detailed shooting script before being on location. Camera operators have to have confidence in me: They won't know exactly what they're going to film before they see the actors play the scene in front of them. Seamus McGarvey, the chief cameraman on *Butterfly Kiss*, had spoken to me about Eduardo Serra. He had been his assistant on *Map of the Human Heart*, which has magnificent cinematography. He told me that Eduardo preferred to use small, very precise light sources rather than the British or Hollywood tradition, which is to light the entire set. It's a less "industrial" approach that suits me well.

Q: Was the historical re-creation a constraint on the mise-en-scène?

A: I was dreading making my first costume film. We started by looking for locations that weren't too constraining, where one angle was great but other ones were impossible. I wanted to have the possibility of moving freely with the actors if they changed their way of thinking or wanted to try other variations. Like a contemporary film in a natural setting. For this reason we traveled a lot: Yorkshire, Scotland, an area west of England, and even New Zealand. As well, he'd written a contemporary story, considered scandalous at the time. To adapt it as though it were a repertory work on the morals of its era would have been a grotesque falsification. Forster's characters work better with this type of treatment by Merchant and Ivory. Sue and Jude, on the other hand, are barely concerned with the clothes they wear, and they don't live in beautiful locations filled with precious objects. We worked hard to make them speak like human beings, rather than characters from a book. They're from modest backgrounds; we had no reason to make them speak in the refined language of the nineteenth century. The re-creation posed other problems. When the little boy is discovered, I had wanted to show the boat and the train on which he arrives, not for picturesque reasons, but because we're talking about industrialization and urban reorganization. This is practically impossible to evoke today, in contrast to the rural world where one can always find a landscape or an old house.

Q: The color work is striking.

A: We took a lot of care here, with the artistic director and the costume designer. The film starts in black and white, the first color sequences are monochrome and the last, in the cemetery, are as well. We avoided green lawns. It's also why we shot Christminster in Edinburgh and not

in Oxford: the setting is described as very somber, cold, dark, and aus-
tere. At the time of *Jude*, I was living in that very area of Oxford: actually,
today it's much improved, warm, and brightly colored.

Q: *Jude*'s intertitles announce the change of location and life.

A: This comes straight from the book. In Hardy's other novels, the characters are rooted in one location. Here, he moves us constantly from
one location to another . . .

Q: . . . another British road movie!

A: Hardy takes Jude from the countryside to the village, not a specific
town, but a sort of mobile, impalpable urban universe. When one starts
the book, mobility is felt as a bringer of hope, giving the illusion that he
can become part of this new society, that it's accessible. But in the end
one feels that it's precisely the absence of roots that destroys the characters: What happens to them couldn't have happened within a community. It's his own ambition for escape that enables the tragedy.

Q: Your films tackle the rejection of society and the rebellion that follows.

A: The characters have this social marginality, but it's not deliberate. It's
not the result of a revolt. In fact, they're trying to join society and live
their lives there, but it doesn't have a place for them. Paradoxically, the
only thing they want is to be accepted as they are. They aren't revolu-
tionaries. What I am more interested in are people who are excluded
from society rather than those who consciously want to change things.

Q: In your first three films, you changed screenwriter and chief operator
each time.

A: Frankly, it's a coincidence! There's more continuity than there seems:
I worked with Frank four or five times before *Butterfly Kiss*; before *Go
Now*, I made *Cracker* with Jimmy McGovern. I hope to work with Eduardo Serra again. For *Butterfly Kiss*, our limited means dictated a slightly
different configuration: As soon as we had the minimum amount of
financing, we had to shoot really quickly and we needed technicians
available right away.

Q: Several words on *Sarajevo*?

A: It's an original screenplay by Frank Cottrell Boyce. When we started
writing, the war was in full swing. The central story is sentimental,
"standard" enough, about a journalist who reports on an orphanage in
Sarajevo. He unsuccessfully tries to lobby the government to evacuate
the children. Finally, as his convoy is leaving, he takes a little girl, brings
her back to England, and adopts her. But filming this war interested me.

I grew up with the idea that a new war in Europe was inconceivable. Or that it would be the end of the world in a nuclear conflict. How could it be that a war could break out in the heart of unified Europe, right next to our preferred vacation spots, between Italy and Greece? And that we watched it on the television, warm at home, without doing anything, as if it was like any other television program? I was struck by this famous Yugoslavian documentary series, on life during the siege of Sarajevo; it sharpened my approach, pulling me away from the central story and attaching me to a lot of little stories intermixed with the main plot.

FIR Chats with Director Michael Winterbottom

Roy Frumkes/1997

From *Films in Review*, January/February 1997. Reprinted with permission.

FIR: One can draw similarities between *Jude* and your previous film, *Butterfly Kiss*. I don't know if it was intentional, but the idea of doomed couplings, for instance . . .

Winterbottom: I think there's a connection in the sense that both are love stories and both are about people who are outside of society. I think the key difference is, I hope, that the audience, when they watch *Jude*, are really going to be with him, seeing the world through his eyes. Jude is someone I admire, and I hope audiences do too. In that way I think it's an easier film than *Butterfly Kiss*, where you kind of stayed back and watched the two people. We contemplated *Butterfly Kiss* having a scene where we suddenly realize that Eunice is a victim herself, that Eunice is being brutalized. But we decided we shouldn't do that. She has internalized the violence and condemnation of society to such a point that there isn't a soft side inside her. She is just what she is.

FIR: Could you explain aesthetically why you chose to shoot the opening of *Jude* in black and white?

Winterbottom: What Eduardo, the cinematographer, and I wanted to do was to create a circular feel to the look of the film. Start in black and white, and by the end of the film we're back to a kind of monochrome. Then, within that, we used filters to create slight shifts in color balance, and the costume design was intense and dark . . . So the opening sequence was part of an overall scheme. I guess because it was cut off by ten years from the rest of the film, it also seemed like one way of clarifying that. In a sense, the opening of the film became a miniature of the rest of the film. What happens to the boy Jude is an introduction to what will happen to the man Jude.

FIR: I remember reading *Jude the Obscure* when I was young, having to look up words, and not finding them in the dictionary—they were no longer used or accessible. It was a tough piece of work.

Winterbottom: Perhaps, but I think the themes of the book are very direct and immediate, and that's what attracted me to it. I think it's a story that appeals to young people, because it's about outsiders challenging conventional ideas. And it's a big love story as well. These are things that appeal to you when you're fifteen and sitting alone in your bedroom. In any society there are always going to be those who are outside what's accepted, for political reasons or moral reasons, reasons of their behavior or their ideas, and you will always be able to read that story and understand it. Even if you're in Sweden and you feel that this is a very democratic society, you can still read a book like that and see that Jude is not able to fulfill the ambitions and dreams that he has because of economic and cultural problems.

FIR: You mention Sweden, and that brings to mind the documentaries you made on Ingmar Bergman.

Winterbottom: I'd been working in the cutting room at Thames Television for a couple of years, and then as an assistant to Lindsay Anderson on a documentary about British cinema. It came out of that, and it meant spending four or five months in Sweden watching Bergman films and meeting and talking with the various people who worked with him. It was incredibly interesting to sit through fifty-five films by one person. What's great about someone who has a career like Bergman's is that he worked constantly over a long period of time, and you can get to the point where you can see phases in his work, see themes come back and change. There's actually enough volume that if he does a comedy that doesn't succeed, it's merely a blip in the overall work. You tend to associate Bergman with those chamber pieces like *The Seventh Seal*, and then you realize that those really began in the sixties, and he'd already been making films for twenty years. There's that kind of longevity. Some years he'd make two films in a summer. It was a great situation and one that is practically impossible to achieve. I guess someone like Woody Allen has done the equivalent thing in New York.

FIR: Yes. And he even tried to do Bergman.

An Interview with Michael Winterbottom, Director of *Welcome to Sarajevo*

Stephen Garrett/1997

From *indieWIRE*, 1 December 1997. Reprinted by permission.

After making his film debut in 1995 with the killer-lesbian, road-trip romance *Butterfly Kiss*, and following it a year later with *Jude*, an adaptation of Thomas Hardy's *Jude the Obscure*, director Michael Winterbottom next moves to *Welcome to Sarajevo*, a complete departure from the filmmaker's style and a considerable challenge to audiences wherever it is shown.

Shot on location and intercut with documentary footage, *Sarajevo* brings to vivid life the intensity of war correspondence, and gathers together the considerable talents of lead actors like Woody Harrelson, Marisa Tomei, and Emily Lloyd, all of whom play supporting roles to the story of one man, portrayed by Stephen Dillane, who makes it his own personal crusade to smuggle at least one child out of the devastated city to safety in another country.

Using news journalist Michael Nicholson's autobiographical novel about saving a Sarajevan child, *Natasha's Story*, as source material, Winterbottom and screenwriter Frank Cottrell Boyce have created a film that unflinchingly depicts one of the most horrifying and generally ignored wars of the late twentieth century.

indieWIRE: Secretary of State Madeleine Albright has seen the film, hasn't she?
Winterbottom: That's right, and now there's a screening for President

Clinton. And I think that Albright said that anything that makes people think about Sarajevo is a good thing, especially since the [American] troops are supposed to leave next summer. So they're beginning Congressional debates soon about whether they should stay beyond the middle of next summer. So I think they kind of felt that anything that reminded people about what it had been like might focus people on the fact that it is worthwhile to keeping the eight thousand troops there to maintain the peace.

iW: Did you ever think that you would be a political filmmaker? Had you considered yourself to be one before?

Winterbottom: I'm always a bit suspicious about that description because I'm not sure, really, what "political" means. I mean, I think these days when the personal is political and the political is personal, it can mean anything, really. So [the usage] tends to be to try and give significance to something and say, "Well, it's a political thing." The aim of this film was really to try and give some sense of what was happening there, to try and show something of individuals' experience of Sarajevo and then maybe from that to build up a bigger picture.

iW: But to have screenings for presidents is quite a change.

Winterbottom: Our hope when we made the film was that it might bring Sarajevo to the attention of people, because the starting point for making the film was a sense of the bizarreness—that here's a war happening in the middle of Europe, we're watching it on television, you can see it every day, and yet we're not doing anything about it—we're not doing anything to stop it. And suddenly when I went to Sarajevo the first time, that was very much the message I got from people we met. It was terrible to go through what they had to go through, but it was made even more frustrating that they knew people could see it and people were watching it as it happened. So in a way, it was a bit like a spectator sport.

iW: What was it like working with the people at the Sarajevo-based SAGA Films?

Winterbottom: It was good. We saw them the very first time we went there, and we showed them the script, and they were about to start filming their own film. But their attitude was: of course ours is a film from the outside, seen through the eyes of journalists coming to watch what's happening. They were making a film from the inside. But they wanted audiences in America and audiences in Europe to see something of what was going on. And so they felt the film reflected enough of their experience to be worthwhile working on. They wanted to be as closely involved as possible. So they were really helpful.

iW: Originally, Jeremy Irons was attached to the project in the main role of British reporter Henderson. How did Stephen Dillane get involved?

Winterbottom: Once it was financed, that's when we really started casting. And we met quite a few people. And certainly by the time we had met Stephen, we kind of felt that, from multiple points of view—from Miramax's point of view, Channel Four's point of view and my point of view—that he was the right person. He had a kind of presence and a kind of questioning, really. When I first met him, he said, "I don't want to do this." And I think he felt nervous because he didn't want to make a film set in Sarajevo which was just about a British journalist. And that was my attitude as well. So I felt he would bring the same kind of balance, the same questions to what he was doing. And all the way through, he was very conscious of trying to make sure that the Sarajevan characters he meets are just as important as his character. And I think that was good in relation especially to Emira [Nusevic], but also to people like the little girl in the hospital, or the baker whose son is in the camp—in all those scenes, it's very easy for the star, for the main actor to drag all the attention. And I think he was really trying to make sure that the other actors got their scene as well.

iW: The title originally was just *Sarajevo*, wasn't it?

Winterbottom: I was sent the book, originally, and a screenplay by someone else, and those were called *Natasha's Story*. When I started working on it, I kind of felt that it wasn't Natasha's story—it shouldn't be just the story of the girl. So we changed it to *Sarajevo*, as a sort of working title, really. Because no one was convinced that people would flock to see it with that title. And then in the film there's a little documentary bit where you see, scrawled on the wall, "Welcome to Sarajevo." So that became the preferred option. Some people did feel that we should just take Sarajevo out of the title altogether, but I felt that the idea of the film was so much about the things that were happening in that particular city, and to try and make people think about not only the characters in the film but all of the people that live there. And it would be wrong to suddenly lose that connection altogether and pretend that it's just a film about journalists.

iW: That's the nice thing—for the first half or so, the film is so many people's different stories; and then it just centers on Emira's story. It was an unexpected turn when I was watching the film.

Winterbottom: Frank [Cottrell Boyce], in writing the screenplay, it was almost like short stories, like chapters in the film. And the central thread is Henderson, but you should go off and see other people and then come back to him. And generally we wanted to have a jagged rhythm and as many surprises as possible. Because living in Sarajevo, one of the worst things would be never knowing what was going to happen next—never being sure where the sniper was and where the mortar was coming from. And so that sense of not knowing where the bullet's coming from, in a way. We tried to put that into the storytelling as well. Part of working on the screenplay was to watch as much as we could, so we watched hundreds of hours of news archives, documentary footage—anything we could from Sarajevo—and we incorporated specific scenes into the screenplay. For instance, the mortar that lands in the bread queue: we'd seen that material, that was an incredibly powerful sequence. It was one shot and it was really the news cameraman running from one person to another and back, almost in a circle—and you could see the cameraman was incredibly panicked and didn't know what to do. And then the sniper started firing and the cameraman was running for his life. Having seen that, I just felt that this has got to be in the film somehow. So we got our [fictional] journalists to go and witness that, so we could include [it] in the story. And we had to recreate it as well. So it was really working from the archive footage. And the general principle was that if we can use the real footage, then let's use the real footage and recreate as little as possible.

iW: Were there a lot of stories which didn't make the final cut?

Winterbottom: Certainly there were lots of stories that we wanted to have in the film which didn't get in: stories that we'd seen on the news and some stories that we did film—and then there were just too many. I wanted to make sure the film had this sort of energy and pace and compression that I felt the screenplay had. And I didn't want it to be huge and sprawling. The first cut was three hours of incidents, so we pulled it down to something where you could cope with it and still get the sense that there were thousands of other people who should have been in the film.

Michael Winterbottom:
Welcome to Sarajevo

Liza Béar/1998

This interview was first published in *BOMB Magazine*, no. 62 (Winter 1998) and is also reprinted in *Beyond the Frame: Dialogues with World Filmmakers* (Praeger, 2007), by Liza Béar. Reprinted by permission.

Lancashire-born Michael Winterbottom's directorial bravura was first noted in his debut feature *Butterfly Kiss*, and subsequently in *Go Now*, featuring Robert Carlyle as a man coming to terms with multiple sclerosis. His latest achievement, *Welcome to Sarajevo*, unlike Srdjan Dragojevic's *Pretty Village Pretty Flame* or Emir Kusturica's *Underground*, views the horrendous Bosnian conflict from the diverse perspectives of a cadre of international journalists covering the Sarajevo siege. It provides a rare dramatic insight into the dynamics—and ethical dilemmas—of war reporting. The American freelance "loose cannon" approach, personified by Flynn (Woody Harrelson), is juxtaposed with the more closely coordinated tactics of a British news team. Amidst rival disasters relentlessly competing for coverage, each reporter or producer must make daily judgment calls about what constitutes "a good story," and strike a balance between observation and personal involvement, between the demands of the job and basic human decency. When the Ljubica Ivezic orphanage, a growing number of whose members are war casualties, is bombarded by artillery fire, the film narrows its focus to the plight of those children and reaches critical mass over a British journalist's promise to a young girl to evacuate her. The means by which he does so, and the ultimate consequences of his action, limn poignancy with suspense.

Shot on location in the immediate aftermath of the Bosnian hostilities, *Welcome to Sarajevo* is based on *Natasha's Story*, a veteran war correspondent's firsthand chronicle of his own experiences. After covering wars for twenty-five years, Michael Nicholson felt obliged to abandon a pure observer stance and to intercede on a human plane in the life of a Bosnian child, whom he took home and adopted. Earlier this year the film, which stars Emira Nusevic as the child and Emily Lloyd, Kerry Fox, Woody Harrelson, Stephen Dillane, and Marisa Tomei as reporters, premiered at Cannes and Toronto. Michael Winterbottom called me in New York from the bustling cafeteria of Soho House, London, while taking a break from auditions.

Liza Béar: What stage are you at on the next film?

Michael Winterbottom: Actually, I'm editing it. It's called *I Want You*.

LB: Sounds like a change of pace. Is it a romantic comedy?

MW: No, it's quite romantic, but it's dark. It's about various people who're obsessed with other people. There are four [main] characters. It's set in an English seaside town, Hastings, which is a resort but also a fishing town. That's why we chose it. It's completely different from *Welcome to Sarajevo*.

LB: At what point were you when the script for *Sarajevo* arrived on your desk?

MW: It was December '94 and the war was still on. Everyone in England was very aware of what was happening, feeling confused, really, that there was a war going on in Europe in the first place. I was born in the sixties, and I'd grown up at a time when war in Europe was seen as history, and everything was very stable. So it seemed strange that the war was happening at all, and then doubly strange that it didn't seem to affect things in England that much. Of course you saw it on the news, you thought it was terrible, but it actually didn't make much difference. Because you'd thought of wars in Europe, the First or Second World Wars, as the most important thing in your life. Even the Spanish Civil War. Everything you read was about people going off to Spain and writing about it.

LB: Like Hemingway.

MW: Exactly. Whereas you were reading about [Yugoslavia] every day but it didn't connect. So when I saw the script it seemed like a chance to find out what was really happening there and make a film about it.

LB: So it had been bothering you for a while.

MW: But only in the way it bothered everyone.

LB: Well, I'm not interviewing everyone. I'm interviewing you!

MW: [laughter] What I'm saying is, I don't feel I had a special connection. I was aware of it, but also feeling disconnected as well.

LB: Where did you grow up?

MW: In Blackburn, Lancashire, a small industrial town in the north of England.

LB: You studied English at Oxford, but didn't become a writer.

MW: No, I can't write. I like reading. It's much easier than writing. Then I took a post-graduate film course at the University of Bristol, and another film course in London. At the same time I was a trainee editor at Thames Television. And then I got a chance to work with Lindsay Anderson on a documentary about British cinema that he was making, and after that I made a documentary about Ingmar Bergman. I wasn't really ever a journalist. Then for three or four years I directed a detective thing called *Cracker* for TV, which I think is being shown in the U.S. I also did a Roddy Doyle series called *Family*.

LB: So the plight of the journalist in *Welcome to Sarajevo* wasn't something you'd been agonizing over because you yourself had been in a similar predicament.

MW: No. Not at all. And I hope how the film works is that what the journalists feel and experience is a more acute form of what everyone can feel and experience. It's not specific to them. They're in the quandary of being right there, and not being able to do anything about it, but that's what everyone feels when they watch on TV what the journalists have witnessed firsthand. The original screenplay was more particularly about one journalist and his adopting a girl.

LB: The screenplay was based on the book, *Natasha's Story*.

MW: Yes, written by Jeffrey Case. I read the book as well, but I wanted the film to be about lots of characters, not just one. So that's when Frank Cottrell Boyce came on and we started working on another draft of the screenplay together.

LB: He's a longtime collaborator of yours?

MW: Yes. I met him briefly at [Oxford] University and then he wrote things I did for television.

LB: Had you been to Sarajevo before?

MW: No. It wasn't clear whether it would be possible to shoot in Sarajevo, because the war was still on at the time. We worked on the screenplay at the beginning of '95.

LB: When did the war end?

MW: The peace agreement was in December '95. When we finished the script it was about May '95. I had already agreed to make *Jude*, based on the Thomas Hardy novel, so I went away and shot that and finished filming it in January '96, and by that time the peace agreement had just been signed. That's when we first went to Sarajevo, January '96.

LB: What was it like making the film in immediate postwar conditions?

MW: Well, obviously there are practical problems. When we first went there it was very hard to telephone from Sarajevo. Roads weren't great. It used to take about two days to get there because you had to drive in from the airport in another part of Croatia. The water supply . . . We had to clear land mines. That was the only real danger. We had to be careful. But there was no war going on once we were filming. The situation was relatively stable. In fact, the main problem was persuading the financiers that it was safe enough to film there.

LB: Did they make you get extra high insurance?

MW: Yes, and we also had to do some interiors in Macedonia because they wanted to know whether we had somewhere else to go if we couldn't go on filming in Sarajevo. It was like an extra insurance policy. Channel 4 developed the screenplay. They had agreed to finance half of it, and then Miramax came in before we started filming. The budget was $6 or $7 million, because we had to go to so many places. It was quite expensive from the travel point of view.

LB: Did you rely a lot on actual news footage of the war?

MW: Actually, there's only about ten minutes of news footage in total but it feels like a lot more because it's interspersed throughout the film in very brief moments.

LB: How did the cast come together?

MW: What was interesting about the situation [in Sarajevo], was that the journalists come in from outside and they're constantly meeting the local people. The script called for lots of children who had to be Bosnian and therefore had no experience acting and no English in most cases, and a lot of them were refugees. So they were essentially being themselves. Then we had to have Bosnian, British, and American actors. Inevitably it was going to be a strange mix of cast. Quite an unusual range of experience and approaches and cultural backgrounds.

LB: I wondered how you picked the actors . . .

MW: I'd seen Kerry Fox in Jane Campion's films and also she'd done some British TV. I was trying to find a mix of people who'd be interesting together.

LB: How did Woody Harrelson get involved in the project?

MW: We had the character called Flynn already [the American free-lance journalist], and when we took the screenplay to Miramax he was already supposed to be "the star!" We already had the line, "No one knows about Sarajevo in America, but everyone knows me." The script required, in a perfect world, someone who could deliver that line and be believable, and it was lucky that Woody had seen *Jude*—Miramax had arranged for him to see it—and liked it. We met up in Berlin very briefly. At the time, he had just done a few films back to back and wasn't really looking for a film, but the subject matter, the fact that we were going to film in Sarajevo, must have persuaded him it would be an interesting film to work on. Having someone as known as Woody was great because his image and reputation mirrored the image and reputation that journalists were supposed to have in the film.

LB: Other than British and U.S., wouldn't there have been French and German and Italian journalists in Sarajevo?

MW: We wondered about it, but in fact, especially from Frank's point of view writing it, it was difficult enough to imagine the Bosnians' experience as well as the British and the Americans' and we felt the script had enough range. Every nationality had journalists there. But the film already felt as if it was lots of people's stories.

LB: You didn't want it to be too fragmented.

MW: Yeah. And adding another culture to the mix would have been difficult.

LB: *Natasha's Story* was written by a journalist who'd been covering wars for twenty-five years, so he was quite a bit older than your Henderson character, who seems more like thirty-five, thirty-six—your age.

MW: Probably it was subconscious, I felt more comfortable with that age. We thought Stephen [Dillane], who'd done mainly theater in England, would be great for the lead and therefore went in that direction. But [in the casting] we looked at actors older than Stephen as well. Also, we weren't trying to imitate the book. We decided quite early on it was just a question of what worked best dramatically. And it felt like the character should be someone at the peak of his career, still ambitious, old enough to be a senior journalist, which he is. Henderson is close to forty and perfectly capable of being the main foreign correspondent of a TV station, yet he's someone who still has a lot to lose. He wasn't like someone who was about to retire anyway and was disillusioned simply because he'd been through it all and had enough. If anything, there was more at stake than if the character had been a lot older. But the basic thing was that we'd met Stephen and thought he'd be great for the part.

LB: How did you meet him?

MW: We'd seen him in a Beckett play at Donmar Warehouse in Covent Garden.

LB: Do you yourself have any ambivalence about the role journalists play in society?

MW: When they do surveys of the least trusted profession, journalists always get the worst ratings from the public. What was interesting about Sarajevo was that obviously it was a very dangerous situation and journalists were risking their lives, and a lot of journalists were killed. But also a lot of journalists became very committed to the story, leaving aside their individual morality. There was a lot of reporting in England which said, we're showing what's happening, and also, something's got to be done to stop it. Newspapers like *The Guardian* and *The Independent* were running real campaigning [advocacy] stories saying, the government must do something, everyone's sitting by and watching this happen and it's terrible. So journalists were fulfilling the true role of the journalist which is to show you what's happening in the world, show you are connected to those events and that some action should be taken. I like the fact that the film is about a very moral bunch of journalists. The Flynn character that Woody Harrelson plays seems much more frivolous and lighthearted than Henderson, the English character, but in the end they're all doing the same job which is getting the stories out of Sarajevo. I like that.

LB: It seems that we go through cycles. During Vietnam, journalists were seen as heroes, as in *The Killing Fields*, which Chris Menges shot.

MW: Watching all the documentary material of Sarajevo, there were numerous occasions when you see something terrible happening. Someone's hit in the street. Someone's shot, a shell goes off. The next second, there are twenty-five photographers taking pictures of someone as they die. It's a complicated thing. But equally, if you don't have people taking those pictures, you never know about it. For people watching that, the first reaction is horrific: How can those people just come and take a photograph of that person instead of doing something about it? But equally they have to get the picture. There's no way of resolving that contradiction. As a film crew going in after the war, we felt a little uneasy being a Western film crew, bringing in all those resources we needed to make the film into a city which had just been through a terrible war.

LB: And suffering from economic disaster.

MW: Exactly. But in doing that we worked with a lot of Sarajevans. Any money that gets spent there is a good thing. Nevertheless, you still feel uncomfortable about it. I'm sure from a journalist's point of view, being in a city where this was happening, that unease is even more extreme because people are getting shot all around and they're relatively secure. They fly back out, they have their flight jackets, they have their armored land rover.

LB: They're still privileged.

MW: Yeah, relatively.

LB: In the film, Henderson actually has two moral crises to go through: fulfilling his promise to Emira to get her out, and once he does, whether to return Emira to her mother or not. Was that in the original story?

MW: What happened with Nicholson the journalist in the original story is exactly what happened to Henderson in the film: When he got back to London with Emira, he realized there was a mother and he therefore had to get adoption papers. When we were working on the script there were suggestions that we should drop that second half of the story. The traditional climax of the film would be: the journey out of Sarajevo, and having got Emira out, that's the end of the film. She's safe; he's got her; he's done the heroic thing. It always felt like that would be too pat, a distortion. If it worked, that sense of him returning to Sarajevo and having to face up to the mother, and having her give her blessing for what he'd done would be more interesting and truer to the situation. We tried to avoid reducing it to one act of heroism, like "save the girl." We wanted to make it more psychologically true, so that he gradually falls into doing what he does. It's not a big dramatic moment where he suddenly sees the light and is converted and then takes action. It's more that he's drawn and sucked into it. And it's only once he's committed to Emira that he realizes the implications, and one of them is going back and getting Emira's mother to agree he's done the right thing.

LB: How did you achieve the incredibly disorienting effect of being at war in the first ten to fifteen minutes of the film?

MW: A lot of things I do are for half-thought-about reasons because it feels right. War in Europe is something I'd been taught as history, it wasn't going to happen in my lifetime. Seeing these images from

Vukovar that could have been the total destruction of the town—it was hardly possible for me to believe it was happening. So at the beginning of the film, to take the image from black and white to color . . .

LB: Took it from the past to the present.

MW: Yeah.

LB: The jolting hand-held camera movements were really unsettling too. You literally don't know where you are, things are coming at you from left and right.

MW: One of the experiences of going there was to see the incredible jumble of contradictions—when you go through a town trying to imagine, where was one side, where was the other side. It was an integrated place originally. One side of a block of flats would be completely destroyed, the other side would be completely lived in. I wanted to get that across, that war isn't a big great homogeneous whole, it's more like lots of weird events. One minute everything's quiet and you can be having a drink in the bar and the next minute, someone's shooting at you in the street. The more jumbled up and contradictory I wanted things to appear, the sharper the cuts between shots.

LB: I suppose your sense of place and direction, of being able to get from A to B, is totally shattered when shells explode and great chunks of physical matter disappear.

MW: For instance the flats that Risto, the translator, lives in the film—a guy who took us there showed us how at different times during the war he would sleep in a different room. At one point he'd think, this room is safe, there can't be any sniper fire here, and then suddenly there'd be sniper fire there one evening, or in the next room or the next room. It was impossible to tell where the danger was coming from because they were completely surrounded by sniper fire, you'd never know which was the safe direction. We wanted to capture what it was like to live there through that.

Winterbottom Walks through Wonderland

Jasper Rees/1998

From *The Independent* (U.K.), 22 November 1998. Reprinted by permission.

The producer Steve Woolley was once asked to compare the American and British film industries. He said it was like the difference between the NASA program and a couple of old women in the outer Hebrides knitting jumpers.

Michael Winterbottom—*Butterfly Kiss, Jude, Welcome to Sarajevo*—is knitting a lot of jumpers at the moment. I met him at Goldcrest's offices in Soho, London. In cutting room 206 the final touches were being put to *Old New Borrowed Blue*, a romantic comedy Winterbottom shot this summer about a French Romeo who comes to stay with his old pen-pal and her husband in Belfast. In room 209, the daily rushes of *Untitled Love Story*, an ensemble piece about a weekend in the love-lives of three sisters, are being given the once-over. It's lunchtime, and Winterbottom still has nine hours of filming ahead. He has the pink flush in his cheeks of the perpetually hurried. When he talks, words tumble out, clattering into one another in a manner that suggests either impatience, or a hyperactive mind, or both.

But that is not why he is slightly late for the appointment, which has taken so long to fix that it almost felt as if I had been trying to get a movie off the ground, not an interview. He nipped out to film a brief snippet for a tribute to Alan Parker. You couldn't imagine two less similar British filmmakers: one a graduate of ads, blandished by Hollywood; the other a distinctly European graduate of television documentary and drama. They have both filmed works by Roddy Doyle. For the outstanding BBC series *Family*, Winterbottom even inherited many of Parker's crew from *The Commitments*. The younger director turned in a much more swirling, brutal account of Doyle's Dublin than the old lag did.

I had met Winterbottom before, in July, on the set of *Old New Borrowed Blue*. A Belfast kitchen had been synthetically reconstructed in the laboratory conditions of Pinewood. There's nothing so cumbersome about *Untitled Love Story*. It is being shot throughout south London with a nimbleness unimaginable to the Hollywood space program.

The roving crew is small enough to flit between locations in a couple of vans, and on set the only people in the room, apart from the actors, are Winterbottom, the cameraman, the sound man and the first Assistant Director. It is film-making pared down to a minimum. "The idea is it's all hand-held, there are no lights, it's 16mm film, we're in real places: in that sense it's like a documentary. It's like an improvised way of filming, very simple in preparation."

The film was originally called *Snarl-Up*; it may be changed to *Wonderland*. They haven't decided which title more accurately encapsulates London. In the meantime, the latest film to have dropped off Winterbottom's conveyor belt is *I Want You*: it is set in a ghost town at the end of the line on the south coast where, Winterbottom says, "the sea acts as a barrier and a gateway."

The film follows a man who returns from prison after nine years to force himself back into the life of his hairdresser girlfriend. But while theirs is the central thread, the town as a whole is seen through the eyes, and heard through the ears, of Honda, a gawky, mute fourteen-year-old refugee from the former Yugoslavia who lives with his sister, a nymphomaniac club singer. Honda has the antisocial habit of eavesdropping on conversations with a listening device. A budding director? "Absolutely," says Winterbottom. "There is an aspect of voyeurism to being a director. Part of the long rehearsal period was the actors in character going off, doing what they would normally do, and me listening on radio mikes to them, recording them in a similar way to Honda. In the film you don't find out anything about the characters. The film is organized almost like a song, with the repeats, the echoes, the choruses. The idea was that the film could work that way; that you feel like you have been emotionally involved but you wouldn't be able to tell someone that much about who Martin or Helen are."

The star of the film, over and above a cosmopolitan cast, is the townscape itself, played by an amalgam of Dungeness and Hastings. It looks like Warsaw-on-Sea. Hardly surprising, as Winterbottom hired Krzysztof Kieslowski's favorite cameraman, Slawomir Idziak, to peer at England through Honda's eyes. "He is Polish, so he likes to look at Britain a different way. When he agreed to do it we particularly watched *The Double Life of Veronique*. What he was doing there was using some of the same colors and distortion of images in the background to create a sense of someone who's got a very partial and limited connection with the real world."

This is a regular trope in Winterbottom's work: the familiar as viewed anew by the outsider. It isn't just a question of asking actors, as he does in almost every film, to bed down with an alien accent. The script of *I Want You* is by Irish writer Eoin McNamee. *Untitled Love Story*, which takes a frank look at modern London, is written by Laurence Coriat, a French woman. And the whole point of *Welcome to Sarajevo* was to encourage outsiders to engage with actual tragedy in a not-so-distant land. For *Old New Borrowed Blue*, the tables were neatly turned on Winterbottom: Northern Irish scriptwriter John Forte says he was "very keen on having a non-Irish director to bring something extra to it."

Winterbottom is himself a native of Blackburn. His father worked in a factory; his mother was a teacher. "When I left school," he says, "I was desperate to get out. But I think that's not to do with the place: when you're growing you feel like you want to do things and escape where you're from."

His reading of *Jude the Obscure*, about an autodidact whose dream of academic fulfillment turns to ashes, seems to have powered his exit to Balliol College, Oxford (known as Bibliol, Christminster in Hardy's novel). "Certainly as a teenager I felt an identification with Jude the outsider. There's a bit where Jude says, 'Maybe not my children but my children's children will be able to go.' Hardy was prophetic, and I felt I could try and go there now."

The subsequent opening of doors to Winterbottom has been such that, at thirty-seven, he is working on his eighth feature-length film. But however fascinating a director he is to a selective audience, the crossover hit is proving elusive. *Welcome to Sarajevo* should have made the breakthrough, but perhaps there was something in Miramax's squeamishness about leaving the place name in the title. For all its sinuous exploration of desire, *I Want You* won't be the one with which Winterbottom goes global; *Old New Borrowed Blue*, with Christopher Eccleston and Dervla Kirwan, sounds like his flightiest entertainment yet.

He turned down the chance to make a big-budget adaptation of John Irving's *The Cider House Rules*. "I felt the script wasn't right and I would rather not make it on that basis than go ahead because it's going to be a big film and it will have lots of publicity." It is now being made by the director of *My Life as a Dog*. But he is still planning to make *Kingdom Come*, a wintry western about the gold rush, which has fallen through once before. This week his regular producer Andrew Eaton went to Los Angeles to check on Gary Oldman's availability.

"Obviously when you make a film you hope people are going to go and watch it and enjoy it," says Winterbottom. "But that's not a priority when I look at a script. I'd rather make a film that appeals to me. The one that doesn't appeal to me but appeals to someone else—you can't make a film on that basis."

Michael Winterbottom's *Wonderland*

Anthony Kaufman/2000

From *indieWIRE*, 28 July 2000. Reprinted by permission.

In Michael Winterbottom's wistful family portrait *Wonderland*, starring a cast of stellar U.K. thespians (Gina McKee, Molly Parker, John Simm, Shirley Henderson, Ian Hart), the British director does for South London what *Short Cuts* did for Los Angeles. Ten ordinary characters in search of an exit, looking for meaning and contentment against the backdrop of London's everyday sights—the Southwark Bridge, the Elephant & Castle roundabout, the Brixton cop shop—banal places somehow made familiar, vibrant, and beautiful.

A sense of community suffuses this South London universe, culminating in a fireworks show where the illumined faces of strangers provide a humanity not seen since the children of Francois Truffaut's *400 Blows* gleefully watched their puppet show. Referencing the French New Wave is not such a stretch for this grit-inspired flick; shot on the fly for just under $2 million with handheld cameras on 16mm film, it owes more to "cinema vérité" than British kitchen-sink realism.

Director Winterbottom expounds on his already eclectic career, from his adaptation of *Jude the Obscure*, to his acclaimed war drama *Welcome to the Sarajevo*, to his upcoming goldmine epic love story, starring Wes Bentley and Milla Jovovich, formerly titled *Kingdom Come*. (For a deeper look into that production, their website is not to be missed, www.kingdomcomemovie.com, which includes call sheets, rushes, continuity lists, virtual tours of the set, notes from the production team, editing stats, and now a voting area to choose the new title—*Sierra Nevada* is currently in the lead.)

Winner of Best Film at the British Independent Film Awards, *Wonderland* was originally owned by Universal when it premiered at the 1999

Cannes Film Festival; it eventually ended up in the laps of USA Films, who have been putting off the release for many months and are finally opening it today in New York and Los Angeles. From Cannes, Winterbottom spoke to *indieWIRE*'s Anthony Kaufman about the working class, shooting handheld, the lush Michael Nyman score, and happy endings.

indieWIRE: There's a tradition of British films looking at the working class in the U.K.; what was your take on it with *Wonderland*?

Michael Winterbottom: The film isn't about the material conditions. It's not an essay on the plight of the working class. I don't want these people to be explained so much by economic things; I wanted to go beyond that. The world of the movie is just like the world I live in, in London. Part of the attraction was just to get on film what it's like living there at this moment. So I don't see a picture of London in the film as being this alienating or alienated, bleak wasteland. I think for me, they're all just struggling to find some connection with other people, struggling to not be lonely, to have someone in their life, to love someone, to be in touch with their parents or their children or whatever. That's the same for everyone.

iW: How did that relate to you shooting 16 mm handheld? Did you ever consider shooting on video?

Winterbottom: We did think about video. I wanted it to be widescreen, which was one issue. But also, if you shoot on video and show it in the cinema, when you watch it in the cinema, it's quite visible, it's quite a heavy technique. I just thought it would be too much of a barrier between what's happening in the film and you watching it. I didn't want to advertise the technique as much as when you shoot on video. Obviously, the 16 mm is very soft, and we shot X-chrome sometimes, so that's even softer, and because we had no lights and we're shooting at night, it's quite grainy. We were aware of that happening, and we did a lot of tests on it, but even so, I still feel it's a softer thing than a video-to-film transfer.

iW: Was it mostly natural light?

Winterbottom: It was all available light. Sometimes, during the night interiors, they would change the light bulb and put a brighter light bulb in. But we didn't have any lights with us.

iW: Were you thinking at all about Dogme 95?

Winterbottom: It wasn't a question of following Dogme. The thing was, we have all of these characters' stories, but I also wanted to try and make connections between them and the people around them, because part of the story is that there's seven million people and you're this individual and you're one of the small group and how that feels. So we wanted to capture moments of ordinary people in the film. In the beginning of the film, in the bar, we went to do some tests without lights, without boards, without microphones. We shot there and they didn't pay any attention to us. As soon as we put a small light up, everyone was very aware. So what we did was try to find exactly the right places for the story to happen, shoot at the right time for the story. Like in the bar we had to wait until everyone was drunk and it was closing time and shoot very quickly in and amongst what was happening and try to capture those moments. The cafe, where [Nadia] works in the film, is just this little cafe in Soho. We didn't do any design to it. The other people that worked there were the real people who worked there, the people who are in the film are people who came in that day to have lunch. We tried to just be three people in the corner and not control the set.

iW: So I read your D.P. is from a documentary background?

Winterbottom: Yeah, he hadn't shot any fictional stuff before. In fact, originally, he did a lot of news war films, and he'd only been in documentaries for a couple of years. What I liked when we did tests in Soho was he would just be right there and completely unfazed about it, because that's what he does all the time—because that's his job all the time. We talked to other feature film cameramen, and I just sort of felt that it would become a mere stylistic thing. They were interested in the idea of 16 mm and grainy, and all this other stuff, but they weren't really interested in this idea of just trying to watch and find something. And what Sean [Bobbitt] brought, because he's a documentary guy, is that when the actors were doing different things each time, he was used to the idea of trying to capture the moment, and trying to find the bit that's interesting. I felt that with the other people we talked to, it would just become a stylistic thing; I didn't want it to be a stylistic thing. Sean was always trying to be at the right place at the right time, so that involves a camera movement. I think his handheld is amazingly steady. Nothing is wobbly-cam, that wasn't the point. We wanted to change the way we were working, rather than just [use] it as [a] device.

iW: Some of the best moments in the film come from the documentary footage with those great scenes with the crowds, all those wonderful faces . . .

Winterbottom: I love those moments. That's why we wanted the music, as well, to try to connect our characters to all those people. And all those people and all the characters, connected to some sort of internal life where there's some dream they all have. I love it when they're playing bingo and they're so absorbed or when they're watching the fireworks and they've really forgotten themselves completely.

iW: Was the Michael Nyman music always intended to be so integral to the film?

Winterbottom: I love this music. Obviously, when you're choosing Nyman, you know the territory you're moving into. We were trying to make a film about the everyday and I was really interested in finding very everyday events, almost nothing dramatic, and still make a film that's interesting. Because the nature of the way we were shooting, and the story itself, these are not people who reveal themselves. They don't tell each other what they're thinking. They don't suddenly open up; we don't have the big dramatic scene where everything's resolved. I didn't want to think that because it's that sort of film, let's not have any music, because it's very documentary and very everyday. I wanted to try and say that their dreams and aspirations are just as rich and powerful as anything else. You can feel like you can have a great, big score, rich and lyrical, and actually, it's appropriate for them. So in the beginning of the film, I feel like it's, Wow, there's this film, and there's this music and for a while, you play it in the gaps, in the between, as punctuations. And then gradually as it goes on, for me, at the end, with the baby or particularly when she says, "Alice, like in Wonderland," it's like yes! There, [it fits] absolutely. [Laughs]

iW: It happens in the audience's mind, too. You may not get the Alice reference in the beginning, but then in that scene, the light bulb just pops on.

Winterbottom: That's why we put the title in the end. Because [if] we [had] done that in the beginning, they would have found the title really ironic, which wasn't really the idea. Because irony suggests that it's just about the real world being bad and "wonderland" is just an ironic comment on how horrible the world is. And I don't see it like that. I think they're still dreaming of some other place, where they are fulfilled, where they do have someone to love, so I wanted to wait until the end because it's a little bit more open about how that connects to the different people you're seeing rather than in the beginning, when you think it's all shit.

iW: The ending really seems to come together on a very optimistic note. Was that your intention?

Winterbottom: I do see it quite optimistically. That was something that developed partly through the shooting. The script, you could interpret in lots of different ways. It was very open as to who those people were. The script probably had a slightly darker feel than the final film. And that was just something that developed, I think, the choice of the casting and who those people were. For instance, Molly and Eddie, once we had them, they were much warmer characters than they originally were. There was a possibility that Eddie's fucking off was going to destroy that relationship and somehow, when we did it, it somehow didn't feel right. You should feel that they should come together more. I do think it's optimistic, but in the sense that they are all struggling. They've all still got possibilities. Obviously, the shape of the film is only one weekend, so there is no definitive answer at the end of the weekend. But I feel at the end of the film they're all still battling away, which is a good thing. It's like the music. By the end, for me, I feel that music is the right music—that it's their music and that makes me feel more positively towards them. As you get to know them more, you get more into them; you understand them better and that is what, in a way, makes it feel more optimistic, because you feel like you've known these people.

iW: After making such an intimate film, how do you see yourself comfortably working on larger-budgeted films in the future?

Winterbottom: The film I want to do next is called *Kingdom Come*, which is a Gold Rush love story with a $20 million budget. In a way, it's not a studio film, but it's still halfway. I don't think I'd ever want to go beyond that, to be honest. I can't see doing what you would call a mainstream studio picture. [Smaller films] are the most enjoyable to work on. If you could work in the way that we did on *Wonderland* or a more conventional way, but on that same level of budget and still get distribution, that would be good. The problem is, if you make a small film and two critics don't like it, it's like, what was the point of that? I just made a film for a year and only ten people are going to see it.

An Interview with Michael Winterbottom: *The Claim*

Damon Smith/2000

Previously unpublished. Reprinted by permission of the author.

Q: Why did it make sense for you, as a British director, to take the story of *The Mayor of Casterbridge* and relocate it to the American West in 1867?

MW: The starting point for what me and Frank [Cottrell Boyce] and Andrew Eaton, the producer, wanted to do was make a film about Europeans going to America, rather than wanting to make a film about *The Mayor of Casterbridge*. So it seemed to us as Europeans perfectly legitimate that we should make a film about the experience of being an immigrant. And really from that point, the idea [was] of the first generation going out to the gold rush. In a way, everyone going to California was an immigrant. And then twenty years later, the next generation in a sense making California part of the project of the railroad. Connecting the West to the East Coast was the idea of connecting the rest of California into the idea of America. And we liked the idea that the young characters in the film would be Americans and the older characters immigrants. Which immediately sets up what I think is a kind of classic thing, with immigrant families being separated not just by generation, but also by their nationality and culture. And with that, it seems like you have the potential to connect the whole immigrant experience in general and specifically in California at that time.

Q: Were you attempting, in some way, to retell the myths of the American frontier?

MW: Certainly, when reading about the building of the railroad and reading about the pioneers going out to California, it seemed like an incredibly exciting time. A time when California—well, Mexicans were there before, but very few Mexican settlers. So the people arriving at the gold rush were this huge influx. People went into this place [at a time when] the population was far less than that in the whole of California before then. There were incredible extremes in terms of survival and physical endurance. And the journey itself to get there was so huge and the continent at that time was so empty. But that was an attraction [for me], the idea of these people sort of like small characters in this vast landscape. And at the same time, if you go to a place where there are no preexisting structures of law and order and society, moral choices are more individual or seem more individual. You're faced with the idea of what is acceptable and what isn't acceptable yourself. That was attractive for the story we wanted to tell and *The Mayor of Casterbridge* then fed into that. The idea of, you know, you do this thing which is obviously a terrible thing but somehow, maybe in that [historical] context, it's more believable, in a way, more understandable than the original context Hardy writes about.

Q: I'm thinking especially of the final image, the aerial shot over the heads of the miners fighting for the spoils Dillon has left behind. How did that fit into the moral framework of the film?

MW: I think it's possible to look at most people's actions in different ways, in different lights, and certainly in the case of Dillon I didn't want him to be entirely the villain, you know, the person who's sold his soul for gold and therefore is beyond redemption. At the same time, when you read the accounts of the pioneers and gold prospectors, it is this very exciting thing of risking everything, of risking your life and risking your fortune. Although that is an adventure, it is basically an adventure motivated by avarice. It's motivated by the desire to get rich and to get rich quick, which is a recurring desire in all cultures. Perhaps that's particularly associated with California and with America in general from a European perspective. So it seemed at the end of the film that it was appropriate in a way that you have one version of Dillon, which is Dalglish saying he was this hero, he was like a king. Then you have a reminder of the other version of Dillon, which is this man who is kind of driven to—not bad acts—but acts of desperation in order to get rich. That is the fundamental driving principle of why people went to California in the first place.

Q: You shot *The Claim* under fairly harsh conditions in Alberta, on Fortress Mountain. What were the rigors of shooting under these circumstances, and how do you think it affected the outcome of the film?

MW: Well, we wanted the film to be as realistic as possible, and we wanted the actors to try and get a sense of what motivated the characters. We also needed there to be snow for the whole filming. It became apparent quite early on that we'd have to film in the middle of winter. We'd have to film quite high up, so in the end we found a place that we thought was just about practical, although it was very touch-and-go about whether it was possible to build there and whether it was possible to do the filming there. But we found a place seven thousand feet up. We had to start building in September, I think it was, because we had to get the foundations in before the ground froze and it got too cold to build. And then we built through to Christmas, and we shot from January to April when the temperatures were regularly minus twenty-five. It was difficult from a practical point of view because it wasn't clear when we started whether we'd actually be able to build the village up there. But then you think, well actually, the original pioneers were building towns like that with their shovels and pickaxes! Just getting their gear around there [was tough]. We had to ask the same questions they probably had to ask, about is it possible to survive here and is it possible to do this, but it was a good thing for us to understand more of what they faced. From the actors' point of view, we said to everyone, "These are going to be the conditions, you aren't going to have the usual luxuries of your Winnebago," and so on. "You are going to be up a mountain and in the cold and it's going to be hard work." And for the actors who agreed to do it, that was an attraction in a way. And it meant that the people who agreed to do it wanted to try and experience, to a certain extent—obviously it wasn't as bad for us as it was for [the pioneers]— but to experience something of the physical extremes. If you are living in those conditions and you are struggling to survive, that affects who you are and how you behave.

Q: So you knew well beforehand what you were getting into. Did you have any hardships that were harder to foresee?

MW: There were days when everything that was built was blown down because the winds were running at seventy miles an hour. I remember the first time we took a camera up there, the first time the cameraman had been up—and he loved it—but we literally couldn't stand. The wind was blowing that fast, and we had to just lie down because it was a complete whiteout. By that stage, the infrastructure was in. The filming was obviously quite cold, but practical. [We were] about an hour and a half south of Banff in the Canadian Rockies. We built for six months, and filmed for three. So it was a long haul. We didn't want the film to be pretty, but wanted to move from being very close in with the people, close in the town, trying to get a sense of the effort of life under living conditions like that, the struggling and the way in which faces show [the strain of the environment]. Then you just have a moment when you stop and look up, and you see this fantastic landscape. You get the sense of isolation and also a sense of the beauty of the place, and then it's back to the effort of trying to live in those conditions and move between those two ways of experiencing the landscape.

Q: What specifically inspired you during the course of filming *The Claim*?

MW: People got there with nothing but what they could carry. It was inspiring to watch the struggles of the crew to build up in the valley and the hard work it took to create the physical existence of the town. And that was the thing that was most powerful about making the film.

Q: How did the Web campaign around the film help the project along, especially in terms of feedback?

MW: One of the films I really love is *Heaven's Gate*. I read the book about the making of *Heaven's Gate* which, I don't know when it was, but it was probably like seven years after the film was made. And it seemed to me like, well, we're going up a mountain, it's freezing cold, it's seven thousand feet up. You know, it's quite complicated but no doubt there will be things that happen we wish weren't happening. And maybe [I should write] some sort of diary of that, which is available as it happens rather than two years later, [when] you tell a story that conforms to what the end of the project is.

Q: You've been very active since making your feature debut with *Butterfly Kiss* in 1995. There was a steamy noir, a modern London slice-of-life fantasia, a melodrama, and recently, the docu-realistic war film *Welcome to Sarajevo*. How do you connect the dots?

MW: They're just stories that interest me. In the case of *The Claim*, it was a matter of sitting down with Frank and our producer and talking about ideas. And gradually we came to the idea of [the gold rush]. Is the story interesting? Do I want to work on this for a year, is the effort inevitably required to make the film going to feel like it's worthwhile?

I'm not trying to impose any other pattern than that. Whether there is a pattern or not, I'm not sure. From my point of view, it's a question of trying to find films I'm interested in.

Q: This is the second time, following *Jude*, that you've adapted a Hardy novel. Do you have a special affinity for his writing, his worldview?

MW: *Jude the Obscure* was one of my favorite books as a teenager, and I love the idea of Jude as a character, really, as an outsider and someone who's defeated, but in a sense because he feels that he's right. He was right to try and get an education, he was right to be in love with Sue. Even though he's defeated, his conviction that he's right stops him from being broken. I like the idea of someone who clutches victory from defeat in the end. Hardy had the ability to transform ordinary people and everyday situations and the world around him into almost mythic [dimensions]. He transforms stories that could be domestic and narrow into something universal.

Q: Questions about authorship and voice are inevitably raised when someone takes a close look at a director's body of work, especially by auteurists. Your voice is harder to locate in that sense, since you've adopted a variety of styles and approaches.

MW: Well, I don't know if that's necessarily the right way to look at films. For a start, films are collaborations, so a film isn't a film by one person, it's a film by a hundred people. You can look at films that are connected through actors, writers, cameramen, or the original books they come from. You can look at films that are about the same subject or films about war or films about family life or films about the nineteenth century or the West or whatever. So I don't think you necessarily have to categorize films by directors. If you have dreams as a director, you don't want to be worried about how your dreams will be interpreted. If you're having the dream, you don't necessarily want to be analyzing them. I don't start off with a particular end product or message in mind, or feeling like I must do a film now that exposes things, or that is more political or more social. I look for the logic of the story to point the way toward how the film should be made. It depends on the nature of the story, the people you're working with, writers, the actors you're working with, et cetera. Everyone contributes to the idea of how the film should be. I think it's more interesting to bring a fresh approach and an open mind to each film, rather than being like, "Well, this is how I make films and I always make films the same way."

Q: The scene in which Dillon's house is hauled across the frozen land-scape seems to be a direct reference to *Fitzcarraldo*. In terms of influences, who else has left an impression?

MW: There's a slight reference to Herzog in pulling the boat over the river in *Fitzcarraldo*. Generally, the major European postwar cinema is where [I look]. The connection between New German Cinema, the French New Wave, and neorealism is the idea of people going out and trying to do things as simply as possible: telling a story but allowing for things that are accidental and that happen by chance, so [you get] that kind of freshness those kind of films have.

Q: Michael Nyman has now worked on two film scores for you. Before that, he had a long relationship with Peter Greenaway, who used to edit according to the music. How does Nyman's evocative style suit the films you've made with him—*Wonderland* and *The Claim*—especially as they're a bit more restrained?

MW: Well, I think they're two different cases. With *Wonderland* the basic idea was a weekend in the life of a family in South London. It's not the obvious thing for Michael to score because one of the things I think he's brilliant at is creating very rich, quite romantic scores. And the idea with *Wonderland* was to juxtapose his music with material that perhaps might ordinarily have a more documentary feel to it. And I wanted the film to have some connection with their inner lives in the sense of what their dreams might be or what their hopes for themselves would be. And I think Michael's music gave that dimension to the characters. By the end of the film, you kind of feel what they'd gone through that weekend is somehow connected to the emotions of the music. I really enjoyed working with him, and when we [were] discussing *The Claim*, we started off with the idea that *fado* would be the music Milla [Jovovich] would sing.

Q: Why *fado*?

MW: *Fado* is like Portuguese blues, and we wanted to have [her sing them] as this character who comes from another culture, and who chooses to become an American by building the town. I think in America people have found a way to transform themselves from being whatever they were when they arrived, to becoming American. Like a lot of folk ballads, they tell the story of typical [homesickness]. One of the things I was reading about was the black miners and generally the pioneers out in the West, prostitutes in the saloons and the tobacco shops where people would come and gamble their money away. All accounts say how sentimental everyone was. Everyone was thousands of miles away from home, whether they were Americans, Europeans, Australians, or Chinese. Everyone was in this vast wilderness, really, and therefore everyone was moved by any poetry or song about home. So you would have miners sitting there streaming in tears, then go outside and shoot someone. That strand of Victorian sentimentality was incredibly strong back in the West.

Q: Tell me about your next project, *24 Hour Party People*.

MW: Well, it's the story of Tony Wilson, the boss of Factory Records, which is a Manchester-based record label. And it starts in 1976. He was the first man in Britain to put all the punk bands on TV. So it starts with him putting all these punk bands on TV, and from that he started a record company. And really the idea of the record company was that they should have no rights over the bands. They put all their money in, making it sort of a cooperative venture, quite idealistic. And over the course of the next ten years, they have bands like Joy Division, which became New Order, along with bands like the Happy Mondays that were big crossovers in dance music. But he also opened Hacienda, which was the main club in England at the time. So it gives you a sense of the whole kind of explosion of ecstasy and dance music in the late eighties, and then how it all went completely wrong. Everyone spent so much money on drugs and they all went bankrupt. But in fact, at the end of it all, a bit like *Jude* at the end of the film, they had a great time and they'd do it all over again, and that's the story. Comes out next year.

The Film Factory

Simon Hattenstone/2002

From *The Guardian*, 29 March 2002. Copyright Guardian News & Media Ltd 2002. Reprinted by permission.

Michael Winterbottom looks a little miffed when I ask him how he has managed to make so many films in so little time. "I don't make that many films," he says, defensively. Oh come off it, you're always at it! He tries another tack. "Most people make a lot of films," he says. Which is blatantly not true. We're lucky to get a film every two years out of British stalwarts such as Leigh and Loach—and they're the prolific ones.

I tell him it's meant as a compliment, and he relaxes. "One reason I make quite a lot is . . . one thing that's quite hard to do in filmmaking which in music you can—it's inherent in the process—is to work with a small group of people, collaborators."

His words tumble from his mouth, in hopeless fragments, like so much scree. He's extremely bright, likeable, and interesting, and he can't string a sentence together for toffee.

If we're talking about prolific, he says, he'd cite one of his all-time heroes—Lindsay Anderson, the legendary director who gave him his first break. Anderson was anything but prolific, I say—he made a couple of great films in an eternity and then snuffed it. Precisely, Winterbottom says.

"Lindsay was a hero of mine. His films were great, but watching Lindsay argue for six months with, say, Wham's managers . . . he loved the conflict, he loved being the outsider—not only in his attitude to the establishment but also deliberately fucking around and pissing people off." So, he says, he learned a very important lesson from Anderson—how not to do it.

He names another hero—Ingmar Bergman, who provided a more useful lesson. After working with Anderson, Winterbottom spent six months in Sweden trailing Bergman for a documentary. "There you have the opposite: a small group of collaborators who worked together and he would maybe direct three plays in the winter, run the theatre company, write the script for a film in summer—sometimes he'd write two scripts for summer—then he'd edit them in the autumn. Bergman wrote and shot fifty-five films or whatever, as well as his main career being in the theatre, and he did that because he had a small team of collaborators and there was no finance-raising whatsoever. He didn't make *Star Wars*, he made 'four actors in a room,' so the cost related to the audience."

Winterbottom has a new film out next week—*24 Hour Party People*, a suitably bonkers biopic of the Madchester years when Factory Records redefined music with Joy Division, New Order, and the Happy Mondays. Other Winterbottom films include the lesbian heist movie *Butterfly Kiss*, his impressionistic portrait of London life, *Wonderland*, his western *The Claim*, his war film, *Welcome to Sarajevo*, and his adaptation of Hardy, *Jude*.

He is a promiscuous genre-hopper. Subject-wise, his films have nothing in common. And yet there is a recognizable Winterbottom style—a studied messiness, a desire to move between film and video, to confuse and explore. He tends to make the gritty poetic, as in *Wonderland*, and the poetic gritty, as in *Jude*.

24 Hour Party People very loosely follows the Bergman template. It is written by long-term collaborator Frank Cottrell Boyce, and produced by Andrew Eaton—the team. Winterbottom grew up in Blackburn, and the bands featured in the film were the soundtrack of his youth. He was also attracted to a story about Factory Records because it closely reflected his own unlikely philosophy—artistic anarchy combined with a Protestant work ethic.

The film shows how financial incompetence helped kill off Factory Records. Tony Wilson, the owner, was a corporate know-nothing who didn't even own the music rights to his bands. Yet at the same time, you can't help admiring Wilson—he didn't own the rights because ownership was against the spirit of the whole adventure: he was in it for the love, not the money.

It's an attitude Winterbottom empathizes with. As far as he is concerned, too much money, too much corporate input, destroys the final product. The beauty of a Winterbottom film, like a Factory record, lies in its spontaneity. He says he hates the idea of perfection and neatness.

"I like things that are not entirely coherent and consistent." At times, say in *Wonderland*, it works in his favor—the end result is a quite beautiful mess. In *24 Hour Party People*, the approach is not quite so successful—the film is unsure of its tone and ends up more *Spinal Tap* than the proud tribute to a heroic failure that he'd envisaged.

But again, that's part of the philosophy—go with your instinct, and before you have time for regrets you're on to the next movie. Working as part of a team enables him to be prolific. "As a director, if you're working with lots of different producers, you're always wondering, 'Are they going to get the money now?' and they're always thinking, 'Are you going to go off and do something else or not?' People wait six months, then they jump ship and try to get other work. The gap between films for many directors is not because people are spending five years polishing the script; it's hanging about getting the money."

Winterbottom loves the European system, used most effectively by the likes of Bergman, Fassbinder, and Rohmer, where the money made by the last film is enough to finance the next film. The problem with Britain and America, he says, is that it is all controlled from the top down, by financiers who know everything about accountancy and nothing about the film-making process. If you make a successful film, you're given twice the budget for the next one—"and when you make a box-office turkey, you're sent all the way back down the snake and have to build up the budget all over again."

Has Winterbottom never been tempted to make a big-budget film? No, he says, and then he remembers he has done—kind of—and he didn't enjoy it. The original budget for *The Claim* was £25m. "It ended up being £15m, so it was the biggest budget I'd worked with, and the one where the shortage of money was the most problematic. In the end, we had to take twenty pages out of the script the week before we made it to try and make it shootable. It's like we can make a film at £2m and shoot the script, but at £20m we have to cut the script by twenty pages." He stops dead, still baffled.

Winterbottom's film company is called Revolution Films. I ask him why. "Well you've got to call it something," he says sheepishly. "No, it would be great to make revolutionary films, but . . ." He embarks on an intricate argument with himself about what a revolutionary film would be, and the possibility of making one. "If you want to be political, you have to do something in the mainstream, something that is going to affect a number of people. Something like Ken Loach's *Cathy Come Home* was bold in terms of the way it was made and the story it told, and it had a big audience because it was made for TV. But look at Ken Loach's stuff now: it's less bold and has a small audience and doesn't have as explicit a political agenda. You can't do the stuff he was doing then. I grew up watching his stuff on TV and I thought it was brilliant and radical."

As he was watching Loach films, he also became a political activist. He remembers campaigning for Jack Straw in his first election in Blackburn, and then when the Labour party saw he was selling the newspaper *Militant*, they threw him out of the room despite the work he'd done for them. "I remember sitting in the Labour headquarters in Blackburn and there was a guy who drove a bus, a well-known local activist, and two of Jack Straw's mates from London were up there, and this guy—every night for fifty years, he'd been out campaigning for the Labour party, and he left the room, and these two other guys were going on about what an idiot he was because he was a bus driver from Blackburn and they thought they were so clever, and he was so stupid. And that's what's happened to the Labour party—it's just full of people who don't really have any connection with the people they're supposed to represent."

These days, Winterbottom dismisses himself as "one of those terrible people who moans from the sidelines and doesn't actually do anything about it." But there is more than one way to be political. For his next film, he is going back down the £2m route—he's off to Pakistan to make a film about Afghan refugees trying to get into London. He admits it's not the most commercial project. "Is it going to play in multiplexes? No, obviously not. Is it going to play anywhere? Probably not. But the point is it will be interesting to do, and if you've got something interesting to do, then why wouldn't you want to do it? I want to do what I want to do rather than what's good for my career."

Anarchy in the U.K.: An Interview with *24 Hour Party People* Director Michael Winterbottom

Jeremiah Kipp/2002

From *Filmmaker*, 6 August 2002. Reprinted by permission.

You could pick any member from the rogue's gallery of characters that inhabit the mad Manchester music scene of *24 Hour Party People* and make an entire movie solely about them. They run the gamut of being fiercely independent, brilliant, hilarious, larger-than-life, and even heroic.

There's the foppish television personality, Tony Wilson (Steve Coogan), who doubles as a record company impresario and compares the emergence of punk to the heyday of Renaissance Florence; the drug-addled troublemaker, Shaun Ryder (Danny Cunningham), who pioneered a new wave of dance music with his band the Happy Mondays; and the troubled young intellectual, Ian Curtis (Sean Harris), the lead singer of Joy Division, who took his life at age twenty-three.

Director Michael Winterbottom's new film documents all of them and more, yet the true protagonist of this vivid collage is the music that emerged from the industrial city of Manchester. The idealistic team that comprised Factory Records, including not only the bands but also the committed producers, managers, and visionaries who brought it about, fused their political and artistic sensibilities (and a dash of cheekiness) to create a voice for the youth culture of Britain and changed the face of pop music.

Following a timeframe that charts the dawn of punk to the death of acid (1976–1992), these rock 'n' roll visionaries are swept up in the party scene they created. Culminating in the infamous Hacienda Dance Club where the beatification of the beat reached its peak, their downfall comes hand in hand with their uncontrolled, hedonistic lifestyle. Whether their quixotic dream brought about a playful revolution or merely self-destructive indulgence is left up in the air. As Tony Wilson says in the film, "We do things differently in Manchester. We let people make up their own minds."

There's logic amid all that chaos, which might also describe Michael Winterbottom's diverse body of work. He made a disturbing impression in 1995 with his brutal "killers on the road" psychodrama *Butterfly Kiss*. His follow-up, *Jude* (1996), brought a sense of immediacy to the period film through his rigorous visual approach. The hand-held camerawork, making use of long takes, jump cuts, and an impulsive curiosity, became Winterbottom's signature in films like *Welcome to Sarajevo* (1997), *Wonderland* (1999), and a haunting western set against the backdrop of the California gold rush, *The Claim* (2000).

Never one to sit still, Winterbottom is already working on his latest project, *The Silk Road*, with locations in Iran, Pakistan, and Turkey. But while working on *The Claim* in the northernmost regions of British Columbia, Winterbottom felt drawn to making a movie closer to home. *24 Hour Party People's* enticing club nights in Manchester were fifteen minutes from the suburbs of Blackburn, where he grew up. "It was something I felt I knew, without having to think about it that much," Winterbottom reflects. "This was about the music I was listening to as a kid. The characters in the film, from bands like New Order and the Happy Mondays, were a part of my generation. It's good to have that time remembered."

JK: When you and producer Andrew Eaton initially discussed making a film about music, you chose Tony Wilson and Factory Records as your subject. Did you share an enthusiasm for those bands and that time in Manchester's history?

MW: That was part of the attraction, being able to put all these fantastic songs in the film. The Factory attitude was essential, dealing with ideas like anarchy, chaos, letting people do whatever they wanted to do. They were in it for the fun, and didn't treat it as a business. That was the big appeal, really. I remember Tony Wilson being on daytime TV at that time, doing the local news. It had always fascinated me that he had this entire double life running Factory Records and being a part of the nighttime music scene. If we had made the film about another record company, it wouldn't be the same.

JK: *24 Hour Party People* covers an expansive time period. What was the starting point for your research?

MW: The first thing we did was meet with Tony Wilson and talk about the basic idea, because without his approval there was no film. We met a few times and he gave us hundreds of anecdotes. He was brilliant about putting us in touch with other people, too. Manchester is a big city, but the music world we were dealing with is quite small and everyone knows each other. After interviewing everyone we could who was actually at Factory Records or the Hacienda, or were in any way involved, we wrote a draft of the screenplay. That was sent out to pretty much all the real-life characters we mentioned in the script. It was our hope to convey that the movie was a bit of a tall tale, a celebration of these real people and events. We wanted to make people happy with the way we were telling it and not fuck anyone off, even though it's impossible to keep everyone happy. On the whole, especially after we started filming, people gradually got more and more on board.

JK: It must have been a daunting process figuring out the structure, since there's so much information to choose from.

MW: Rather optimistically, I imagined it as a collage of music from all the bands in Manchester at the time, or at least all the Factory bands. We tried to shape things by having the film split into two halves, with the turning point being Ian Curtis's death. The first part follows Tony Wilson and Joy Division, with Tony feeling as though he's on the periphery because he's not part of the band. He hasn't grabbed all his chances that first time around, so he goes overboard during the second half of the film. Things shift a bit when the Happy Mondays show up. Tony tries to join in with that band, so he's doing a ton of drugs with them and things spiral out of control.

JK: In the film, Tony Wilson describes himself as being an observer in his own story. In a way, the music seems like the protagonist—and the characters are there to service that experience.

MW: Most of what Tony says in the film is the sort of stuff Tony would tell us. He does like to hold the limelight, but at the same time would say things like, "The movie shouldn't be about me! It should be about Ian Curtis and Shaun Ryder and [recording studio producer] Martin Hannett. I'm not interesting. The music is interesting." We put that disclaimer into the film, not because it's true but because it's typical of Tony. Obviously, people have their own view of things, and their own attitude toward Tony Wilson. Some people we spoke with would mention him and say he's a cunt, a bastard, a twat, and all this other stuff. In the end, the British advertising campaign for the film had a picture of Ian Curtis with the inscription, "Genius," a picture of Shaun Ryder that read, "Poet," and a picture of Tony Wilson that said, "Twat."

JK: Your story allows viewers to see the importance of people who were not musicians, like Joy Division's manager Rob Gretton (played by Paddy Considine).

MW: When you talk to anyone in Manchester, Rob Gretton is a huge hero. No one has a bad word to say about the man. Once we'd talked with a few people, it became clear he was to be a main character. It's interesting because in the traditional rock 'n' roll film, the bands are creative geniuses and the record company people are the shits that exploit them. I'm sure that's true in many cases, but what was nice about Factory was that it didn't have that shape. We could have characters be people like Rob Gretton who run the record company, and show their enthusiasm for the music. They simply love it. It was a nice irony being able to show the Happy Mondays not giving a shit about the music and just wanting to do loads of drugs. The record company actually cared more about the music than the band did, at least on the surface. It was nice to not tell the typical movie, but that's what emerged from the actual stories people told us.

JK: Does the fast, do-it-yourself aesthetic of video complement a story about the emergence of punk, which had a similar ethos?

MW: You're certainly right that the idea was to make the film in the spirit of Factory, which is essentially the spirit of punk—and although their music isn't punk, that was their starting point. That's what excited them enough to say, "Fuck it! Let's all go off and do what we want to do!" Within the filming, I tried to give the actors as much a sense of that as possible. Using digital video helps, but the key in terms of how we made it was to not use any lighting really, or to only use the lights that existed within the club during those scenes. We would give each of the actors radio [microphones], allowing them to talk at the same time—with two people talking in one corner and two in the other. We'd shoot the entire scene in one go. It was that freedom that motivated us, allowing the actors to roam around and have the camera do what it wants to. That can be done on 35mm or 16mm or DV.

JK: Right, but the entire look, color, and texture of DV is completely different from film.

MW: Video does have a certain look, it's true. At the beginning of the project, we knew there was archive footage we wanted to use, some on tape and some on film. I wanted to have different textures. When our director of photography Robby Muller came on, he was keen to stick mainly with DV. We did shoot a bit of 16mm and 35mm here and there, but on the whole we chose to use DV. We wanted to have different textures within the film where you jump from one scene to another and have a change, rather than it all being seamless. The nature of having many characters over a long period of time seems to suit that, really.

JK: What choices did you make in shooting the different concert sequences? One of the Joy Division songs was done in black and white. And when you recreated the Sex Pistols performance at Lesser Free Trade Hall, the entire scene looks like stock footage.

MW: That's because some of the Sex Pistols scene was lifted from the archival footage, shot on Super-8—or Standard 8, in fact. Instead of a choice about style, it was about finding a certain way to do it if we wanted to use that content. That dictated the entire process of our filming, which was good. It was much better for us to have the Sex Pistols in archive footage from that concert than it would've been if we tried to dress people up and pretend. But that meant we had to try and make the scene around that stock footage seem close enough that you could feel like it's in the same area. The shooting style does change as the movie goes on. With the Happy Mondays, the Hacienda, and the emergence of the rave scene, we wanted more saturated colors as a change from the Joy Division scenes. They are different eras, but the tone is dictated by the nature of what things were like. People wore different colored clothes in 1990 than they did in 1979.

JK: How did you go about making the concert scenes feel authentic?

MW: Peter Hook from New Order lent us bits of gear to help those scenes look right, and Martin Moscrop from [the Factory band] A Certain Ratio was the film's music supervisor. He got the actors to play their instruments as well as they could, even though most of it was done through playback. But by the time we shot those scenes, the actors in those bands could play the songs. We would film the concert scenes with four cameras a couple of times in front of a crowd, taking all the versions of the tracks that we could find. We'd play them out to the PA system on the day we filmed, so we would have the original recording and the PA room recording. Then we'd vary between the two to find a more or less raw sound.

JK: It must have been an interesting process for your actors, since they're playing real people—and some of them are well known.

MW: In terms of casting, there were several constraining factors. You think to yourself, "Do we have to cast someone who looks like that character? Are they able to sing or play a musical instrument? Can they act?" We also wanted to cast as many people from Manchester or Northern England as possible. In the end, we didn't go for look-alikes. But it was interesting, because as we went along they seemed to become more and more like the people they were playing. There was some interaction between the bands and the actors playing them, which seemed to help quite a bit. The actors playing Joy Division and New Order met up with [guitarist/songwriter] Bernard Sumner and [bassist] Peter Hook. Paul Ryder and Rowetta from the Happy Mondays were actually in the film, so the actors were able to hear their stories and get to know what they were like. The great thing about being in a band is you know each other really well, since you start when you're fourteen, fifteen, sixteen, or whatever. By the time you're doing records, you're incredibly intimate and know everything about each other. A film is the opposite of that, where people come together for eight or nine weeks then disappear. To provide an environment for the actors, we tried to make it as much like they were in a band as possible. They all hung out when they weren't filming together and would go off partying every night. There wasn't a lot of difference between their time off set and on. Fortunately, the actors got on well together and still do. I think they all kind of decided that being in a band would be much more fun than being in the film.

World in Motion

Jessica Winter/2003

From *The Village Voice*, 23 September 2003. Reprinted by permission.

On the borders of Afghanistan, that other country where America won the war but lost the peace, a massive refugee crisis grinds on mostly forgotten by the world at large. For prolific British director Michael Winterbottom, however, the situation has occasioned a politically charged road movie. *In This World* is a stark, startling account of two Afghan refugees attempting the perilous trek from a crowded camp in Peshawar to the gold-paved streets of London. A daring hybrid of documentary and fiction that took the Golden Bear at Berlin this year, it even features two real-life displaced Afghans in the lead roles. "The idea was never to come up with characters and then go and cast them," says Winterbottom, "but to meet people and then build a story around them."

The story-building process began as Winterbottom and screenwriter Tony Grisoni visited the Peshawar camps and met with asylum seekers in London. In October 2001, while U.S. bombs rained on Afghanistan, they tried a dry run of the movie's Pakistan-Britain route, gathering more ideas and personalities for the final product along the way. "Even while we were filming, Tony went ahead and met more people who then became characters," says Winterbottom, who shot in Pakistan, Iran, Turkey, Italy, France, and England.

"Everything in the film derived from the stories people would tell us," says Grisoni, who has also collaborated with Terry Gilliam on *Fear and Loathing in Las Vegas* (1998) and the upcoming *Brothers Grimm*. "But the journeys are so fraught with anxiety and danger—they're something to get over, to forget. You'd ask, OK, what happened? And they'd simply say, I got smuggled to London. They'd be very resistant to go through it all again. In the next generation, I guess they'll become romantic stories."

For the voyagers, Winterbottom chose refugees named Enayatullah and Jamal Udin Torabi, who portray refugees named Enayatullah and Jamal. "The criteria were that they had to speak English and they had to be willing to trust us—people from England they'd never met saying, Do you want to come away with us for two months?" Winterbottom explains. "We weren't saying, You'll get a chance to become refugees in Europe; we were saying, This will be interesting and you'll get paid. That said, Enayatullah didn't speak a word of English, and Jamal, you know . . ." Winterbottom laughs, "he decided to come back over here." After production wrapped and Torabi returned to Peshawar, where he earned about a dollar a day in a brick factory, the young man made a second trip to London and claimed asylum. Now sixteen and living with a foster family, Torabi was granted exceptional leave to remain in Britain until his eighteenth birthday.

Thematically, Enayatullah and Jamal's story doesn't mark entirely new ground for Winterbottom and his famously eclectic corpus: In *Welcome to Sarajevo* (1997), set during the 1990s siege, he depicted the resettlement of a young Bosnian refugee in England. But given the dark and lethal turns that *In This World* eventually takes, the ambiguous territory it occupies between fiction and documentary may raise more ethical red flags than, say, the Madchester mythography of Winterbottom's previous movie, *24 Hour Party People* (2002), which played cheeky cat-and-mouse with Factory Records lore. *In This World*'s most horrific episode is based on the deaths of fifty-eight Chinese immigrants who suffocated inside a sealed refrigerator truck traveling to Dover in 2000.

"Some people get quite angry; they want to know for certain what's fictional and what's real," Grisoni concedes. "But that blurring has always been the case—it's more complicated here, but it's been going on since the first time someone turned on a camera—since the workers filed out of the Lumière factory."

"The film does play with what's true and what's not," Winterbottom says. "Take Jamal. He is an Afghan refugee; his parents are refugees; he's young enough that he was actually born in the camp. Most of his family live in one of the camps next door to the one we filmed in. His brother and sister in the film are really his brother and sister. His mum is alive, but in the film she's not, so that is a fictional thing.

"If we wanted to change something, we would, and obviously all the illegal or dangerous events are staged," the director continues. "But usually we tried to create situations where people didn't have to act. We never said to anyone, You should be this sort of person, you should say this, you should act in this sort of way. It was more, Hey, do you want to be in the film? OK, you're going to drive them here and drop them off here, or, They're going to come to your house and you're going to make them a cup of tea."

The patient perpetual motion, the semi-improvisational methodology, and the decidedly hands-off direction of nonprofessional performers all parallel the docu-fictions of Abbas Kiarostami and other Iranian masters, though Winterbottom downplays the similarities. "I like Kiarostami a lot, but then again, there's lots of great German road movies," he says, citing Wim Wenders's *Alice in the Cities* (1974) as a personal touchstone.

With *In This World* only now reaching U.S. audiences (on the heels of Stephen Frears's thriller *Dirty Pretty Things*, set among London's refugee underground), Winterbottom already has his next feature in the can: the nocturnal, near-futurist romance *Code 46*, starring Tim Robbins and Samantha Morton, which recently premiered at Venice. Filming exteriors in Shanghai, Dubai, and Jaipur, Winterbottom used handheld cameras, radio mics, and available light—the same semi-guerrilla technique he deployed to capture the thrum and throb of street life in his bittersweet paean to London, *Wonderland* (2000). "We wanted not to create an artificial world, but to use bits and pieces of the existing world and juxtapose them," he explains, "because the future's more likely to look like the real world today than any studio set you're likely to build."

Code 46 forecasts a global polar divide between heavily checkpointed urban labyrinths and barren no-man's-lands, a time when a person's freedom and livelihood heavily depend on a passport-cum-insurance plan called a "papelle." Sound familiar? "When we started working on the script, I was making *In This World*, and a lot of the texture of *Code 46* came from our experiences in the deserts of Pakistan and Iran, the refugee camps, the hassles with visas," says Winterbottom.

In turn, *In This World* responds to a chronic virulent strain of anti-immigrant scaremongering in right-wing British tabloids like the *Daily Mail* and *Daily Express*, either of which could give John Ashcroft a run for his money in the xenophobia sweepstakes. "Whenever I come across them, I'm always astonished by the huge amount of space given to stories about bogus asylum seekers and people invading our country," Winterbottom says. "It's an obsession. We were lucky with *In This World*—in

Britain it got a lot of press coverage and sparked discussion about immigration, and maybe someone who saw the film would spend an hour thinking about what it's like to be a refugee."

Michael Winterbottom

Sheri Linden/2004

From *The Hollywood Reporter*, 3 August 2004. Reprinted by permission.

Michael Winterbottom's words pour forth in a high-octane rush, a fitting complement to his nonstop work behind the camera. The London-based director's surfeit of creative energy has fueled four films in the past two years alone, and he knows what he wants to do next. In the decade since his striking big-screen debut *Butterfly Kiss* (which premiered in the United Kingdom in 1995), he's proved to be not only the busiest British filmmaker of his generation (he's forty-three) but, in the view of many critics and fest programmers, the most compelling and versatile.

United Artists is readying *Code 46*, a visionary glimpse into the near future, starring Tim Robbins and Samantha Morton, for Stateside release August 6, while the sexually explicit Festival de Cannes entry *9 Songs* continues to stir up controversy. In the midst of all this, Winterbottom and Andrew Eaton, his partner in the British-based Revolution Films, found time to executive produce *Bright Young Things* (ThinkFilm), Stephen Fry's upcoming directorial debut based on an adaptation of Evelyn Waugh's novel *Vile Bodies*, about an eccentric group of socialites in the 1930s.

"You have to have films that you want to make," Winterbottom says modestly.

There seems to be no shortage of such projects for Winterbottom and his core group of collaborators at Revolution, chief among them Eaton and writer Frank Cottrell Boyce. "Lots of ideas come up, so we're usually working on three or four different ideas for films," Winterbottom says, adding that "because we make films quite cheaply, it's easy to finance them."

Next, Winterbottom hopes to direct an adaptation of Laurence Sterne's eighteenth-century experimental novel *Tristram Shandy*. If all goes as planned, the project will reunite the director with Steve Coogan, who toplined 2002's *24 Hour Party People,* Winterbottom's acclaimed valentine to the music-scene heyday in his hometown of Manchester, England.

Winterbottom brought two films to major fests last year. Just weeks after winning the Golden Bear in Berlin for his docustyle drama *In This World,* he wrapped *Code,* which went on to premiere at Venice. While *World* is very much a contemporary, ripped-from-the-headlines exploration of the emigrant experience and *Code* a futuristic love story with a noirish twist, there's an urgent sense of political reality that connects the two pieces.

"They started from a completely different place," Winterbottom says, but he adds that "by the time we made *Code 46,* we were aware of the connections, the social relationships within the film. Having made *In This World,* we drew on that experience to give a texture to *Code 46.*"

Also part of the connective tissue in a diverse body of work is a shooting style that often brings a documentary feel to the proceedings. The use of hand-held cameras and a preference for available light lends piercing intimacy to the working-class family drama *Wonderland,* a 1999 Cannes competition title, as well as to the DV-shot *World* and *Code,* which was filmed mainly on 35mm.

"When we were filming in Shanghai or India," Winterbottom says of the globe-hopping, sci-fi love story, "we could go out and put Tim Robbins and Samantha Morton into the middle of the street and shoot there and be relatively discreet and be able to shoot without too much hassle."

That approach, which aims to make the camera "invisible" while heightening the actors' freedom, plays a crucial role in Winterbottom's controversial *Songs.* Made for a mere £100,000 ($182,000) without outside financing and "done as almost a hobby, a part-time project," the film drew critical praise on its premiere earlier this year at Cannes—and lots of attention for its unsimulated sex scenes, which were part of its raison d'être.

"The movies should be the obvious place where you can see people making love," Winterbottom says. With its capacity for narrative complexity and visual immediacy, he maintains, mainstream cinema should be "where you can deal with the relationship between sex and love in a sensible and interesting way. Films are becoming incredibly conservative about how they show sex." If it receives the British Board of Film

Classification's OK, *Songs* would be the most explicit film ever shown in mainstream U.K. cinemas.

Still, Winterbottom insists, "In one way, it's a concert movie; that was one of the attractions." The re-created Joy Division and Sex Pistols shows in *Party People* made the director long for the experience of filming real concerts—in *Songs*, music alternates with more intimate scenes of the film's central couple.

While his tastes might make Winterbottom the least likely independent director of a studio-based film, he was briefly attached to Scott Rudin's *Freedomland* at Paramount and is discussing another project with the producer. Winterbottom's absence from Hollywood is "not an in-principle thing," he says. "It's a question of the subject, really. Whatever film it is, you have to really feel passionate about it to make it worthwhile in putting that time and energy in."

Michael Winterbottom on *Code 46*: Typical Love Story in an Atypical World

Wendy Mitchell/2004

From *indieWIRE*, 6 August 2004. Reprinted by permission.

Usually, I'd be offended at being offered only ten minutes of interview time with a filmmaker; but with Michael Winterbottom, I almost want to encourage him to stop talking and get back to work as soon as possible. Since his 1994 debut feature, *Butterfly Kiss*, Winterbottom has established himself as one of the more eclectic and prolific contemporary filmmakers. In the past five years he has given us a masterful slice of life of damaged Londoners (*Wonderland*), a Western (*The Claim*), the Manchester music history/comedy *24 Hour Party People*, and the vérité Afghani refugee story *In This World*.

Now Winterbottom returns with his first science-fiction film, *Code 46*, which he made with longtime collaborators Andrew Eaton (producer) and Frank Cottrell Boyce (screenwriter). *Code 46* is set in the near future, when the world is divided into megacities and desert slums, and travelers need special "papelles" (like passports or visas) to travel between cities. William (Tim Robbins) is an investigator who suspects a worker named Maria (Samantha Morton) of forging papelles. They have a brief affair, hindered not only by his family back home, but also a violation of Code 46, the government's law that prevents them from being lovers because of their genetic makeup. The film focuses on their emotional turmoil but Winterbottom also explores life in this futuristic society: viruses that allow for specific feelings, memory erasure procedures, cloning consequences, hybrid languages, and a depleted ozone layer that makes it dangerous to venture outside during daylight.

During our ten-minute chat, thanks to his rapid-fire talking, Winterbottom discussed his team's script collaboration process, twenty-first-century architecture, the challenges of futuristic filmmaking, and more. We didn't make it to my questions about Oedipal themes in *Code 46*, the importance of music in his films, the explicit sex in his forthcoming controversial feature *9 Songs*, or what he's working on now. No doubt we'll find out soon enough.

iW: You've worked so much with [screenwriter] Frank Cottrell Boyce, how does your collaboration process work? Specifically with *Code 46*, did he show you a script, did you come up with the idea together, what was the genesis?

MW: The idea comes up between us really, Frank and I and also our producer, Andrew Eaton, who we've worked with the whole time. Having finished *24 Hour Party People*, we were thinking of things to do and gradually we came up with the idea to do a film set in the future. We talked about it for a couple of months. We talked about the idea of it and the world of it, and then Frank started writing the screenplay.

iW: Is there a lot of collaboration after he starts writing?

MW: Yes, there is. Particularly on *Code 46*. Because Andrew and I were off making *In This World*, about two refugees, we got this idea of people having no papers and trying to travel from one place to another and the problems that creates. And a lot of that world—refugee camps, people in deserts, people outside the system, without papers, excluded—those elements are part of the social fabric of *Code 46* as well.

iW: Are you a sci-fi fan, had you always wanted to make a sci-fi film?

MW: No, not really, I was a bit naïve and innocent. It was a lot of fun starting from scratch: What do we want this world to be like? How does this world work? That side of things was interesting. But from my point of view, *Code 46* wasn't a reference back to many previous science-fiction films or novels. It was looking at the world as it is now and drawing on our experience from different places, especially drawing on the cultures of the places where we were filming. Part of deciding what this world would be like was going to look at locations. We went to Dubai, Kuala Lumpur, Shanghai, Hong Kong, India, and joined up bits of those cultures into the culture of *Code 46*.

iW: Most sci-fi films tend to get bogged down with gadgets or fancy sets, and this was more about human interaction and how society had changed—why was that your focus?

MW: I think that's what interests me generally. If you make a film set now in London or in Pakistan or wherever, the thing that interests me is the relationships between individuals—individuals and society, individuals and their family, their girlfriend or boyfriend, it's all the same idea. Even though *Code 46* is set in the future it's still the same idea, the heart of it is the love story. It's interesting to see the way in which the story of these two particular characters connects with the culture of the film. A lot of the aspects of the world of the film are amalgams of things that already exist . . . It wasn't about creating or inventing anything, it was just "this bit is interesting," "that bit is interesting" and putting them together. Shanghai is the main city but we put the desert of Dubai around the outside of Shanghai. You can juxtapose two elements that aren't together in reality but you can see those connections in a slightly odd light.

iW: Why did Shanghai and Dubai represent the future for you?

MW: It's partly the look. Pudong, the new part of Shanghai, has had this amazing explosion of building in the past fifteen years. This whole city has basically been built in the space of fifteen years, so that whole look was introduced. In Dubai, you have this amazing look of flat desert with nothing and then suddenly you have high rises. It's an artificial, arbitrary kind of building. "Let's build a high rise—not because we're short on space, but because we like the look of it!" But it was more using places for their culture. City versus desert. The controlling of a very hostile climate—trying to green the desert—was something that connected to elements of *Code 46*. Also in Dubai the local population is much smaller than the immigrant population, so it's very multi-cultural. There's the idea of a city being not so much part of a nation, you're not from India or China or America, you live in the city or outside the city, you're in the system or outside the system. You get that feeling in Dubai in a way. Also a lot of the migrant labor in Dubai is from the Indian subcontinent, and those laborers have a different set of rights than other people. You get that sense of a population being used for very functional reasons: people having to leave where they are from in order to make a living. And the great thing about being in Shanghai, as well as it being a lot of fun, was being in this culture that was changing rapidly and being transformed. A lot of the people that we were working with were beneficiaries of the change, but there are other people who have suffered from the changes. The people we were working with are doing things that ten or fifteen years ago would have been impossible. You were working with a group of people in a society that's in a sense very different from the society they were born into. That was interesting and useful and enjoyable from the point of view of making a film where you are imagining a new place and changes. You're working with people who have already experienced those things themselves.

iW: Most sci-fi films have huge budgets to build futuristic sets . . . How did you compensate for not having a huge budget in the way you shot this film?

MW: In terms of crew, I always like to work with the smallest possible crew, because the fewer people you have the more fun it is and the freer it is, the faster it is, and the more interesting it is. So for those reasons, and just for other reasons to do with character and fiction I prefer to take actors and put them in real settings and real locations and real situations rather than create artificial locations that serve the characters. It's just much easier when you are walking down the street with your actors to do that in a real street that's still open with people on it, rather than to close it off and bring in extras. Generally speaking, that would be my approach. So from the beginning, I thought we should do this on location, to go to Shanghai, to go to Dubai, to go to India, instead of just building a studio set. There is a financial side to it but really that's just the way I enjoy working. In the case of this film, obviously because it's in the future it's not as easy to work like that. So a lot of elements were more controlled than normal. Like the interiors, a lot of those were done in London. The building where Maria works, half of that is Shanghai and half of it is in London, and all the people in that building are extras. It's a question of finding the simpler solution rather than the most complicated.

iW: We can't connect with the circumstances that William and Maria are living in, so how did you try to ensure that the audience could get an emotional connection with these people?

MW: You can't really ensure that. You can just try to make sure that the people in the film behave as honestly as possible and react to each other as honestly as possible and hope that people connect with that emotionally. I think we started with a story that's very familiar—you meet someone, you fall in love with them, circumstances force you apart. It's a very banal idea of a love affair, but we put it in the context that perhaps make you look at it again in a different way. You hope by picking good actors that people engage with those characters.

Michael Winterbottom Gets Naked

Stephen Rodrick/2005

On a bleak British afternoon last fall, Michael Winterbottom and his small crew were preparing for filming on the top floor of Felbrigg Hall, a possibly haunted seventeeth-century manor in eastern England. Winterbottom, one of England's most prominent independent filmmakers, was directing an adaptation of Laurence Sterne's often-cited, rarely read novel *The Life and Opinions of Tristram Shandy, Gentleman*, aptly described by the comedian Steve Coogan, who plays Shandy in Winterbottom's film, as "a postmodern novel written before there was a modern." (The cast includes the critically acclaimed British actors Jeremy Northam, Shirley Henderson, and Stephen Fry, all working at scale just so they can be in a Winterbottom film.) Sterne's book has frequently been described as unfilmable, which is precisely what interested Winterbottom. Published in 1760, *Tristram Shandy* is the memoir of an eighteenth-century country gentleman who wishes to share his "life and opinions" but is so overcome by the urge to tell digressive, often saucy stories about his father, Walter (a harmless but eccentric pedant), his Uncle Toby (who rides a hobbyhorse and obsesses over an old war wound), and his own conception (which was botched when his mother asked his father if he had remembered to rewind the clock at the moment of climax) that he barely manages to get to his own birth before the book's end. It features many of the avant-garde flourishes now associated with writers like Dave Eggers and Jonathan Safran Foer. There are drawings, blank pages, and a page of solid black after a beloved character dies. In keeping with the meta vibe, Coogan plays Tristram, Walter, and a version of himself interacting with the film's crew and co-stars. The day's scene had Coogan/Walter leaving the birth of Tristram, walking off-camera and meeting his (Coogan, the charactor's) wife, Jenny, played by Kelly Macdonald, who is breast-feeding their baby, being played by a six-month-old baby named Daisy.

While the set was being prepared, Winterbottom, who often doesn't realize he's mumbling rapid-fire instructions to himself in his Lancashire accent, approached Daisy's mother, who was standing just off-camera, and whispered something to her. She made a startled face and then retreated into Daisy's diaper bag. A moment later, she handed Winterbottom a pacifier dunked in her breast milk. With a naughty grin, he approached Macdonald.

"So, maybe we can just put it down there," Winterbottom said, motioning the pacifier toward Macdonald's bra. "She can just suck on it next to your breast, and it will look better."

The set went quiet as Winterbottom awaited Macdonald's response. Macdonald, a pixieish Scot, initially looked as if she might swoon onto the period furniture, but she agreed. Nearby, a manor staff member tsked her disapproval. A producer from BBC Films girded the crew for an eruption. "I'm a mother," she whispered. "When that baby realizes there's no milk there, she is going to scream bloody murder."

The scene began and, just as predicted, Daisy wailed at speed-metal decibels. She turned a light shade of purple, seeking succor that was not forthcoming. Winterbottom didn't seem to notice. As with many of his films, Winterbottom was shooting this movie, titled *A Cock and Bull Story*, in a jumpy, hand-held documentary style. He burrowed his head into the back of his cinematographer, Marcel Zyskind, moving him into the exact position he wanted. After the scene was finished, Macdonald was near tears, but Winterbottom had a wide smile on his face. "The baby screaming is perfect for the scene, perfect," he said. "One more time."

The atmosphere on the *Cock and Bull Story* set was chaotic and exuberant. Andrew Eaton, Winterbottom's best friend and longtime producing partner—together they run Revolution Films—had just returned from London with news that the film's already bare-bones $3.5 million budget needed to be cut by another $1 million. Simultaneously, Winterbottom's previous film, *9 Songs*, was causing a national furor. The film, which is scheduled to open in the United States on July 22, about one young couple's affair viewed almost entirely through sex scenes, features unsimulated intercourse and the odd bondage and masturbation scene. Earlier in the day, the British Board of Film Classification gave *9 Songs* the equivalent of an R rating, allowing it to be shown in mainstream cinemas. Down in London, conservative members of Parliament denounced the decision as another sign of moral and cultural decay. On the set, the troops were giddy. Eaton, an exuberant Irishman, proudly displayed a text message from his seventeen-year-old daughter: "I am so proud of you, you are changing the world."

Meanwhile, Daisy's mother timidly suggested that it was time for the baby's 4 p.m. feeding. Winterbottom sweet-talked her into submission. "Just one more," he pleaded.

An hour and a half and a half-dozen takes later, the northern sun faded. Winterbottom, filming on digital video and using only natural light, called an end to shooting. Only then was Daisy fed.

Michael Winterbottom likes his fictional films to be as real as possible. Or at least as real as Winterbottom's imagined version of reality. A few years ago, as he was preparing to shoot *24 Hour Party People*, a tartly comic account of the Manchester music scene of the seventies and eighties, the Hacienda, the legendary Manchester dance club that gave birth to rave culture—and where Winterbottom was planning to do a good deal of filming—was razed. Undeterred, Winterbottom re-created the club to the smallest detail. For the frenzied crowd scenes, he recruited Manchester's gangsters, ecstasy dealers, and pimps to stand exactly where they might have stood in the original club. He also dragged Joy Division's original instruments out of storage and gave them to the actors playing the band.

Sometimes the re-creations get him in trouble. Winterbottom's crew had to hastily flee the Manchester airport a step ahead of the law after one take of a scene in which the actors playing the drug-addled members of the band Happy Mondays licked spilled methadone off the airport's floor. Winterbottom had "forgotten" to get the scene approved by the airport authority.

Since then, Winterbottom has taken his realism to more extreme levels. In 2003, he filmed *In This World*, a harrowing refugee story with a cast of actual refugees, which won the British equivalent of an Oscar. Still, despite border squabbles and having to smuggle film out of Iran, *In This World* was merely a prelude for *9 Songs*, a sex story with actual sex. Winterbottom told me that one reason for doing the film was to expose the hypocrisy of the industry. "You can show people eating and doing normal things, but you can't show two people making love, the most natural of all things," he said. "That's insane."

The idea came to him, he said, after he grew frustrated with what he saw as the implausibility of the love affair in his previous film, *Code 46*, starring Tim Robbins and Samantha Morton. "Love stories have too much narrative to make you feel like, 'Oh, that's what it's like to be in love,'" Winterbottom said. "I wanted to make a love story starting with two people in bed and keep it simple. You displace all the energy on a story that proves to be irrelevant to being in love or not. The idea was go to the opposite extreme and see what happens."

Margo Stilley and Kieran O'Brien, the stars of *9 Songs*, met only three days before they first had sex on film. There was a quick get-acquainted session and a slightly longer screen test during which they both read a scene from *Code 46*. On the first day of filming in the fall of 2003, they met again at a hotel in London. First, they helped Winterbottom and his two-man crew haul equipment up to a suite. Then everyone had a cup of tea. A few minutes later, the two actors got naked.

"We shot a scene where Margo and I were just kissing and taking our clothes off," O'Brien recalls. "It wasn't until after lunch that we had sex."

When he first met with Stilley and O'Brien before filming, Winterbottom told them that *9 Songs* would be shot without a script (Winterbottom's films either have no script at all or only a loose one), and little would be explained about their characters, Lisa and Matt, except that she is an American student in London and he is a scientist. The only real break from sex would be the occasional rock concert.

"He told us he wanted to explore a love affair from the point of view of making love," O'Brien, who has worked with Winterbottom on a number of films, including *24 Hour Party People* and *A Cock and Bull Story*, told me. "Nothing would be simulated. I'd trust Mickey with my life, so once we agreed to do it, there wasn't a lot of discussion about it."

Winterbottom and his crew, the cinematographer Marcel Zyskind and the sound coordinator Stuart Wilson, worked on three films together before *9 Songs*, and there's an ease in the way the trio work together; a slight tap on the back moves a camera, an arched eyebrow changes the sound setting. But that first morning there wasn't the customary camaraderie, just the clattering of equipment being set up in silence. While the goal of that day was to see whether Stilley and O'Brien had the physical chemistry needed to make the film work, there was a second objective: find out whether Winterbottom and the crew could stand to witness it.

"At first, everyone in the room was just deathly quiet," says Stilley, who had never appeared in a film before. "It was like, 'Can we really do this, and is this O.K.?'"

After the first awkward undressing scene, Winterbottom strategically retreated. He spent the rest of the morning shooting the couple in non-sexual scenes. He had O'Brien and Stilley dance together, hug in a chair, and read in bed. "I think that really helped us get comfortable with each other and with the crew being there," O'Brien says. "We just got more and more relaxed."

After lunch, the five reconvened and filmed the first sexual encounter. As would happen throughout the shoot, Winterbottom left little to chance. "He really mapped out everything," O'Brien says. "The order he wanted me to take off my clothes, her clothes, whether my socks stayed on or not. He had specific ideas of how he wanted our bodies to move. Sometimes, he would start us and then stop and say, 'Let's try this from a slightly different angle,' and then take fifteen minutes to reset the shot. I wondered if he remembered the delicate machinery of the male sex organ."

The one concession Winterbottom made to the actors was minimizing the time they were actually having sex. "There's a lot of moments in the film where it looks like we have been making love for a half-hour," O'Brien says. "We weren't. Michael would shoot quickly from a lot of angles, and that gives an impression that isn't the reality of what we were doing."

At 7 p.m., the group stopped for the night. After packing up their gear, the five went to a bar and had a nightcap. "Actually, I think we all got pretty drunk that night," O'Brien says. "It was a long day."

While Winterbottom had worked with O'Brien before, he had never met Stilley, whom he found through a casting agency. She was a twenty-one-year-old student in London who was supporting herself as a model. Having a star with no film experience was a plus for Winterbottom. "Actors can be really jaded," he told me. "And it's hard to get past that. I wanted something that was raw and natural. Margo had that."

Since there was no script for *9 Songs*, Stilley and O'Brien arrived each morning of the thirty days of shooting with little idea of what the next twelve hours might involve. Winterbottom would say hello and nonchalantly announce that day's festivities—sex in the kitchen, bondage in the bedroom. "We would beg him, 'Please give us some information just so we can prepare ourselves for the next scene,'" Stilley says. "But Michael doesn't want you to be prepared." (Taking that to its absurd conclusion, Winterbottom and Eaton held three or four wrap parties just so his actors would feel the end was near, even when it wasn't.)

Winterbottom also says he doesn't believe in rehearsals. "If you rehearse and miss filming something real, you might not get it back," he says. "If an actor is going to have to perform in a room full of crew, why rehearse without them there? Why not film everything and increase your chances?"

As shooting dragged on, Stilley found it increasingly difficult to see *9 Songs* as just a job. "The only way I could do it was to be Lisa on and off the set," she told me. "I'd answer the phone as Lisa. My friends thought I was crazy. But it was the only way I could deal with that feeling of, 'Oh, God, what kind of person am I becoming that I'm getting used to this?'"

In January, I met Winterbottom for the American premiere of *9 Songs* at the Sundance Film Festival in Park City, Utah. Stilley was there too, and she still seemed to be grappling with what she had done. (When the film opened in England, the British tabloids staked out Stilley's family's North Carolina home and followed her two younger brothers to school.) At the Egyptian Theater, she paced furiously in the lobby and then bolted from the midnight screening with Winterbottom and Andrew Eaton in tow. After a drink, they returned to the theater for a question-and-answer session and found the crowd equal parts bleary-eyed, mortified, and intrigued. Winterbottom was asked what separated the film from pornography.

"Porn has its own sensibility," he said. "From the way it's shot, to the lighting, to the way the characters look. You watch ten porn films and then watch *9 Songs*, it's pretty clear the difference."

One difference is in Winterbottom's casting. Stilley, while quite beautiful, is a pale, flat-chested brunette, a head taller than O'Brien. And while there is little story to *9 Songs*, unlike pornography, it has a sense of intimacy between the lovers. It's also quite unlikely that any single porn film involved shooting two hundred hours of digital video, as Winterbottom did for this film.

"The variables were so few on *9 Songs*, Michael could structure it out more than any other film," Eaton says. "In that respect, he was in heaven."

I received a quick indoctrination into the Winterbottom School of Filmmaking upon arrival in Blakeney, a seaside village about one hundred miles north of London and base camp for the *Cock and Bull Story* shoot. Jet-lagged and disoriented, I was picked up at my hotel by Eaton. On the drive to the manor, he blared the Scottish band Teenage Fanclub and happily conceded that financing for the film was in flux. If things didn't work out, he told me, he and Winterbottom would be on the hook for several hundred thousand pounds. "Most companies wouldn't even start filming," Eaton said. "That's the mistake. We figure, once you start shooting it's harder to shut us down because the financiers' money is already being spent."

On set, I was introduced to Winterbottom, who quickly returned to shooting. About an hour later, the crew took a break, and Winterbottom, who is forty-four but looks younger, approached me appraisingly. Cocking his head a little to the right, he said, "You know, I think you would be perfect in the next scene." He then explained that the next scene was a nightmare sequence in which Steve Coogan dreams that his co-star, Rob Brydon, is receiving all the attention from the director, crew, and the actress Gillian Anderson. Why not throw a fawning writer wanting an interview into the mix?

Within two hours, Winterbottom had shot my scene a half-dozen times with no coaching other than: "Just ask him like you'd ask anyone for an interview. Don't worry about the words."

Not worrying about dialogue isn't unusual for Winterbottom. For *In This World*, Winterbottom and a five-person crew traveled to Peshawar, Pakistan, on the first commercial flight from England after 9/11, armed only with a bare outline telling the story of two Afghan refugees making the highly dangerous and illegal four-thousand-mile trek to England. Eventually, Winterbottom settled on Jamal, a teenage boy, and Enayatullah, a man in his twenties, for the lead roles. Jamal and Enayatullah had no acting experience; Winterbottom had them play versions of themselves. He provided them with no specific instructions as they traveled from Pakistan to Iran to Turkey and up through Europe. He simply put them into situations and started filming. When you see Jamal leaving his brother in Peshawar, it is truly Jamal's brother, and the goodbye is real. When Enayatullah looks for work in an Istanbul factory to raise money for the rest of his journey, the other workers you see are doing the same. In the end, Winterbottom filmed two hundred hours of footage, largely not knowing what his characters were saying.

"I wasn't trying to do a documentary," Winterbottom says. "The idea was not to make them do something they wouldn't do. We would put them in settings, on a bus, at a border, and just film. I just wanted them to come off as themselves."

As the journey continued, Winterbottom made alterations to the plot on the fly. When Jamal and Enayatullah arrive at the border of Iran and Turkey, the script originally called for the two to be robbed by a Kurdish family. As Winterbottom watched the family dote over Jamal, however, he had a change of heart. "Michael couldn't do it," recalls Stuart Wilson, the sound coordinator on the film. "Not just because they were so nice and friendly, but because it didn't seem real anymore."

Winterbottom has made thirteen films in the last eleven years, despite being legendarily disorganized. Last year, Sabrina Broadbent, Winterbottom's former partner and the mother of his two children, wrote *Descent*, a touching, smart novel in which one of the main characters, a film director, loses wallets, scripts, and relationships with alarming frequency. (Winterbottom lost his wallet at least three times on two continents during my time with him.)

When I asked Winterbottom about the breakneck pace of his moviemaking, he said that he was happiest making films and least happy waiting around to make them. He learned the hurry-up-and-go ethos early in his career. The second son of a draftsman, he attended Oxford before studying film at Bristol University. After graduating, he served as a junior assistant to Lindsay Anderson, the legendary British director, while Anderson was putting together a short film on the pop band Wham! visiting China. Winterbottom watched in horror as Anderson dawdled for a full year on the project, shooting and reshooting interviews, squabbling with the producers, and, eventually, stealing the film from the cutting room when the producers took it away for the final cut. "I was a huge fan of Anderson's, but if you're doing a Wham! video, you have to assume it's for fun or money," Winterbottom says. "He loved to spend a lot of energy on everything but actually making the film. I knew that's not how I wanted to do things."

Winterbottom's critical breakthrough came in 1996 with *Jude*, a stark adaptation of the Thomas Hardy novel that was Winterbottom's favorite book as a teenager. His compulsive drive for realism was already in evidence—a pig-gutting scene in *Jude* features an actual pig being gutted. At Cannes, the film won him a standing ovation and the attention of reviewers and producers like Harvey Weinstein and Scott Rudin. It didn't, however, earn him much money. This, too, is a theme in Winterbottom's career—critical attention without commercial success.

While making *The Claim*, a loose adaptation of Hardy's *Mayor of Casterbridge* (and at $20 million, by far the most expensive of his films), he and Eaton put the film's dailies on the movie's Web site before sending them to MGM/United Artists, which was fronting half the money, and publicly reported their unsuccessful attempts to cast Madonna in the film. On the eve of shooting, the budget was cut by $2 million, meaning that the ambitious plot had to be scaled back. *The Claim* received mixed reviews and Eaton and Winterbottom together lost half a million dollars on the project.

In 2003, Winterbottom directed *Code 46*, the dystopian thriller with Tim Robbins and Samantha Morton. Shooting didn't go smoothly, according to Winterbottom, particularly when Robbins demanded that he have a bodyguard, and that sushi be provided for lunch while shooting in the Dubai desert. Winterbottom, who often flies economy class with the rest of his crew, was not amused. (Robbins declined to comment.)

Both Winterbottom and Eaton gleefully recount Robbins stories and other Hollywood misadventures. They seem to revel in a certain recklessness. When I saw the two at the Sundance Film Festival in January, Eaton invited me to join him and Winterbottom at lunch with Steven Soderbergh to discuss a possible adaptation of Terry Southern's *Blue Movie*. Alas, when I showed up, it became clear this was Winterbottom's first meeting with Soderbergh, who had not been told I was coming. I beat a quick retreat to the bar, leaving behind a sheepish Winterbottom, who had, I noticed, a small dollop of shaving cream on his ear.

While Winterbottom was shooting *A Cock and Bull Story*, Eaton worked the phones trying to set up their next project. "We're talking with Scott Rudin about Michael directing *The Corrections*," Eaton told me. Rudin owns the rights to the Jonathan Franzen novel. "Who knows how it will go," Eaton said with a shrug. "Rudin's a weird guy. It's really tempting. Michael and I are making less money per film than we were ten years ago. We could make some real money and use it to do more of our films."

But Winterbottom has passed on big paydays before. After the Cannes screening of *Jude*, Harvey Weinstein flew Winterbottom to New York on a private jet. Winterbottom went on to direct *Welcome to Sarajevo* for Miramax to generally good reviews, and Weinstein approached him with a script written by two unknowns named Ben Affleck and Matt Damon. He offered Winterbottom $1.5 million to direct the film that became *Good Will Hunting*. Winterbottom declined.

"I just couldn't buy into the premise of what a great hero the Matt Damon character was and how brilliant he was," Winterbottom told me.

Weinstein then offered Winterbottom a chance to direct *The Cider House Rules*. Winterbottom was intrigued. He signed an option to direct in 1998 and went to Amsterdam to meet with the author, John Irving, who also wrote the screenplay. Irving didn't appreciate Winterbottom's criticism of his script, and the project wobbled on through a year of rewrites. Eventually, Winterbottom came up with a novel suggestion: make the film as a trilogy and have the first film end as Homer Wells, eventually played by Tobey Maguire, leaves the orphanage where he was raised. "But Harvey said it was a terrible idea, like I knew he would," Winterbottom recalls. "And that was that."

Weinstein stopped calling. But another well-heeled suitor replaced him. In late 2000, Winterbottom got a call from Rudin, who sent him a copy of the Richard Price novel *Freedomland* and a work-in-progress script. "I told Scott, 'I really love the book, but not the script,'" Winterbottom says. "And then he didn't talk to me for two years. Then suddenly, I started getting calls at 4 in the morning from him."

Rudin's persistent calls renewed Winterbottom's interest, but the two clashed over Rudin's insistence in casting the sixty-something Morgan Freeman for the lead role. "The character was supposed to be forty in the novel and have a twenty-year-old son," Winterbottom says. "It just didn't make any sense. You can't be a director if you think the main character is wrong for the part. So I walked away. I never thought I would hear from Scott again." (Rudin eventually cast the younger Samuel L. Jackson in the part.)

But Rudin and Winterbottom began talking again last fall. For months, the two danced around about *The Corrections*. Then, in December, I received an e-mail from Eaton saying: "Rudin in town, staying at the Ritz. Not returning my calls. Not a good sign." It wasn't. A few days later, Rudin hired Robert Zemeckis to direct the film.

On a rainy afternoon at Felbrigg Hall, a day of outdoor shooting was lost. But Winterbottom was surprisingly cheerful. "I'm sick of shooting all this period stuff," he told me. "There's only so much you can do with it."

Just as much to pass the time as to get something usable, Winterbottom started shooting Coogan and Brydon in their makeup trailer. One of the running subplots in the film is the rivalry between the established Coogan and the upstart Brydon. Ostensibly, the scene is about Brydon, an elfin Welshman, trying to work up the courage to ask Coogan if he can stay at his L.A. pad while making studio rounds.

Winterbottom shot for a few minutes, and eventually the conversation began to wind down. You could feel that Coogan and Brydon were waiting for Winterbottom to tell them to stop. But Winterbottom, his back crammed against a wall of the tiny trailer, said nothing and motioned for them to continue. Then, Brydon stared into his mirror intently and started lifting up his gums and examining his discolored teeth.

Brydon: "I'm getting them bleached."

Coogan: "If you're not playing a character in the Salem witch trials, I would get them whitened."

Winterbottom laughed. "Just keep talking," he urged.

Coogan whispered to Brydon: "Are you sure you want to do this? He's going to use it, and then you're going to be the guy with the teeth."

But Brydon started playing with his teeth again.

Brydon: "I don't think the color is great. What would you call it?"

Coogan: "Uh, on a sliding scale, I'd say not white."

Brydon: "How about a hint of yellow? Barley meadow? Tuscan sunset? Pub ceiling? If you think your teeth are too good, you get bogged down in the leading-men category."

Coogan: "You can sleep easy at night at that prospect. You shan't be."

Brydon: "You see yourself as a leading man?"

Coogan: "I'm greedy; I want my cake and eat it too."

Brydon: "But have you?"

Coogan: "Well, yes."

Brydon: "In the world of Steve you have, but have you really?"

Coogan grimaces. When Winterbottom finally stops the proceedings, after nearly half an hour of shooting, it is unclear whether it is Coogan the character or Coogan the actual human being who is angry. Either is fine with Winterbottom, as long as it is real. "You put talented people in position and try to capture a moment," Winterbottom said. "It's not that complicated."

Chaos Theory: Michael Winterbottom on *Tristram Shandy*

Adam Nayman/2006

From *Cinema Scope*, no. 25 (Winter 2006): 20–23. Reprinted by permission.

With his seen-it-all gaze and embedded smirk, the actor and comedian Steve Coogan carries himself like the living embodiment of British unflappability. It's amusing, then, to see the former Alan Partridge's face scrunch up while discussing his professional relationship with Michael Winterbottom, who has directed Coogan in the two best movie roles of his career: Manchester pop impresario Tony Wilson in 2001's exhilarating punk odyssey *24 Hour Party People* and eminently flappable British comedian Steve Coogan in this year's *Tristram Shandy: A Cock and Bull Story*. Actually, the pair bring out the best in each other: both films rank among the sharpest and most inventive comedies of the past decade.

"He's one of my best friends," said Coogan of Winterbottom during an interview in Toronto. "But I never know whether he's just instinctive—going by the seat of his pants with this vague idea and it just somehow kind of comes out okay—or if he's actually a lot cleverer than that, and just keeps it to himself." I suggested that it would take a clever man to get the ever-aloof Coogan to doff his clothes and dangle upside down inside a giant prop uterus, as he does in *Tristram Shandy*. "By now," Coogan sighed, "I quite enjoy flying in the dark. I've become comfortable when I work with him. Certainly, the people who haven't worked with him before, I see a slight panic in their eyes. Like, 'What is going on here?' And I tell them, 'It's okay. This chaos will somehow work its way out.'"

Chaos might just be the common denominator of Winterbottom's films, which are surely impossible to group together in terms of subject matter. His nineties' output includes a sideways stab at distaff serial-killer pathology (*Butterfly Kiss*, 1995), a Thomas Hardy adaptation (*Jude*, 1996) and a bitter, unwieldy media satire (*Welcome to Sarajevo*, 1997). The Canadian co-production *The Claim* (2000) was a *McCabe and Mrs. Miller*–esque Western—loosely based on Hardy's *The Mayor of Caster-bridge*—that eschewed genre stateliness for bustling hubbub; this bustle was then carried over to the crowded dance floors of *24 Hour Party People* and reached a kind of apotheosis with the hard-scrabble DV camera-work of *In This World* (2003), a sort-of-documentary filmed entirely on location with a skeleton crew following two Afghani boys on their peril-ous underground journey to London.

The film won the Golden Bear at the Berlin Film Festival, but Win-terbottom's other 2003 release, the gauzy oddity *Code 46*, evoked confu-sion: was it a tragic love story, a slab of speculative sci-fi along the lines of *Blade Runner* (1982), or dire sociological analysis cloaked in genre? As it turned out, it was an uneasy mix of the three, and stands as a case of the director's overweening ambition running away with him. Winter-bottom's follow-up, *9 Songs* (2004), was an experimental, non-narrative art film that juxtaposed live performances by contemporary rock bands with explicit sex scenes. It was received with a predictable mixture of excitement, outrage, and puzzlement, especially by auteurists eager to finally stamp the ever-erratic director as a socially conscious humanist interested in indomitable personalities astray in extraordinary circum-stances. Said critics were now presented with a film where the people were little more than props in what appeared to be avant-garde porn—another salvo from deep left field courtesy of British cinema's most reso-lutely unclassifiable maverick.

If *9 Songs* is a paean to passion for passion's sake, then *Tristram Shandy* pays tribute to the process's ostensible aim: it is a movie preoccupied with birth, which would explain the giant prop uterus. Indeed, the novel upon which it is based, Laurence Sterne's eighteenth-century pre-post-modern monster *The Life and Opinions of Tristram Shandy, Esq.*, unfolds entirely in the moments before its eponymous narrator's birth—the joke is that in laboring to provide the reader with thirteen volumes' worth of context about the major figures in his life, Tristram never actually gets around to beginning his own story. He is played in Winterbottom's film by Coogan, who also plays Tristram's father, Walter, and is also, as the film progresses, revealed to be playing himself—that is, he is playing an actor and comedian named Steve Coogan caught in the difficult process of filming a movie based on Tristram Shandy, which is being directed by an affable fellow named "Mark" (Jeremy Northam), who looks and acts an awful lot like Michael Winterbottom, who is of course the real-life director of the entire precarious enterprise.

It sounds onanistic in a Charlie Kaufman sort of way, but it rarely plays that way. Where most films about filmmaking lapse lazily into indulgence, Tristram Shandy is amorphous strictly by design: even its scraggliest curlicues coalesce. The running gag pitting Coogan against his 24 Hour Party People co-star, the much less famous Rob Brydon—who appears in the film as himself, and in the film within the film as Walter Shandy's crippled, emasculated brother Toby—in a passive-aggressive game of actorly one-upmanship dovetails with the novel's depiction of fraternal antagonism; the scenes in which an exhausted Coogan cuddles with his newborn child echo Walter Shandy's unconditional adoration for his son. Watching the usually deadpan Coogan struggle to change his baby's dirty diaper is genuinely disarming, but it's also balanced against a coy throwaway bit in which Northam's Winterbottom manqué notes that a dollop of paternal sweetness might be just the ticket towards humanizing his famously acerbic star.

It doesn't all work—the period-dress re-creations of the novel are deliberately fussy and drag on—but in its best moments, Tristram Shandy is dazzling. The camera seems to float between Coogan and his amorous personal assistant Jennie (Naomie Harris) as they weave their way through a field littered with extras in full military regalia and she speaks of her love for Fassbinder; their escalating flirtation is rendered as a full-on nighttime fugue, and the tone is overpoweringly romantic. It's almost enough to distract us from the surrounding conceptual gag: the extras are gathered to rehearse an expensive and elaborate battle scene that has already been deemed superfluous by Mark and his collaborators.

As it turns out, neither Winterbottom nor his onscreen alter ego have much interest in literal warfare, which fits nicely with the thrust of Sterne's novel: the book closes with one character wondering why we glorify war, but dim the lights during the act of lovemaking. Tristram Shandy is Winterbottom's earnest attempt to hold a candle up to his own professional milieu. The result is that rare movie made in the 8½ mode that's actually about more than its creator's own professional or psychosexual insecurities: it's elegantly worked-out chaos, a full-tilt affirmation of artistic fecundity.

CS: I really enjoyed the film, having wallowed through *Tristram Shandy* in university.

MW: Really? You actually read it?

CS: I tell people I read about 75 percent of it, which is not to say I read the first three quarters.

MW: You can skip through it. Especially when you get these long divergences, and you're waiting to come back into the story.

CS: I enjoyed the first fifty pages so much that as my eyes started to glaze I decided I was enjoying the rest, too.

MW: Well, when Sterne wrote it at first, he only published the first two volumes. Like all books in those days, he only wrote the first two volumes, and then he couldn't get them published. He had to pay to get them published. And then they were a huge success. I'm sure part of it was deliberate—the lack of shape. When he did the first books he probably didn't know where it was going to go either, and after that, it was like churning out sequels—every time he writes a bit more of the book, he gets more money.

CS: When I'd read that you were making this film, I had the same response that's all over the press materials, which is that neither you, nor anyone else, could possibly film this book.

MW: The house that Sterne wrote most of the book in is like a trust now—it's like a museum. And they were very helpful to us. We arranged a screening for them there, and we invited some *Tristram Shandy* experts. They all came and watched it in this little village hall in Yorkshire. And they loved it. What was quite nice for them, I think, is that in a sense, the spirit of the book is to be chaotic and anarchic, and they were quite into the idea that a film wouldn't necessarily have to be exactly like the book to be a version of the book.

CS: I think a lot of films about filmmaking and the creative process are indulgent not on purpose, whereas your film about filmmaking is indulgent and digressive entirely on purpose. It's very meta stuff.

MW: It's very simple stuff, really. We were going to keep as simple a shape as possible. It was going to be about one night of filming, and then we were going to find all the distracting things that can go on around a movie set. It's not even really that much to do with filmmaking . . . it could be anything. It's just a bunch of people. It's like work, or it's like anything in your life: there's never enough time to sort it out. But yeah, most of the stuff in the film is stuff that pretty much seems to happen on every film.

CS: Is it cathartic to do that Sterneian thing, to hold these processes up to the light, as it were, and say, "Yeah, this is really difficult"?

MW: The idea was to turn out something with the same attitude that Sterne has in his book, which is basically that, yeah, these people are stupid, and they're doing stupid things, and they're doing badly and worrying about things that are fundamentally trivial. But you have affection for them.

CS: Was there ever a chance of filming the novel straight?

MW: We had talked about it off and on. The idea originally was to do a version set entirely in the eighteenth century. But the book is not straight. You could never do a straight version. But it was only part way through we decided to move between the two periods.

CS: Did you inventory the book for things that would work well on film, like the passage featuring a single entirely blank page?

MW: It seemed to me that the core of the narrative was the beginning of the book, which is about Tristram's birth, and is a very left-to-right kind of story, starting at the beginning. And it's something that's very easy and direct to understand, because in the scene, Walter Shandy is sort of obsessive, he wants everything to be all right with the birth of his son, he's spent his life waiting for a child. It's something everyone can understand. It seemed like the core. And so when we decided, "Okay, let's do the film about the film itself," we knew that if there were any other little bits from the book that didn't fit into that opening scene, we could just nick back and drop them in later.

CS: Do you enjoy tormenting Steve Coogan with bizarre stunts, like crashing his hang-glider in *24 Hour Party People*, or, in this film, dangling naked inside a large plastic uterus?

MW: Well, in *24 Hour Party People*, the reason we did that is because his character had to see himself as God. So it was fun to hoist him up again, and revisit that.

CS: He trusts you very much in this film. Some people might not understand that what he's doing is skillful self-satire, rather than just being a jerk.

MW: Steve does that quite a lot, and he's brilliant at it. On the Alan Partridge TV chats, he takes things that aren't very far away from Steve and then exaggerates and distorts them. But it is brave. A lot of elements of our story are actually close to things he's done in real life. I think that what he hopes is that if that someone says "I'm Steve Coogan," and shows how bad he is, then you'll think he must be totally aware of all that stuff. A lot of comedians do that. They tend to play quite close to who they are.

CS: Like Ricky Gervais on *The Office*.

MW: Yeah.

CS: The scenes in your film when he's with his baby and his girlfriend— even though I know they're not really his baby and his girlfriend—are very humanizing, and very touching.

MW: When we were working on the screenplay, we talked to Steve about the scene where he goes up to change the nappy, that it would be nice to have a little moment like that. And Steve said that if he was going to do something like that, then he would have to immediately spoil it by going down and announcing to the other characters that he'd done it, that he'd changed the nappy, like it was some great thing.

CS: Can you clear something up for me? In the very last scene, was Kelly McDonald's hair different? I know that she plays Steve Coogan's girlfriend in the film, but in the last scene, it seemed like she looked different and was out of character, and actually just Kelly McDonald the actress.

MW: I kind of liked the idea that there would be slightly more of that kind of pulling back, away from the fictional crew. Like you're saying, Kelly McDonald is not Steve Coogan's girlfriend, but the idea was to try to be playful. And there are actually moments when you see the real camera crew, and not the fictional camera crew. There was also a TV crew making a documentary about the film, and at one point we were going to pull even further back and include them.

CS: Is this one of your usual "it's for the DVD" things, like the extra material in *24 Hour Party People*?

MW: We generally have a lot of DVD stuff, yes.

CS: Is *9 Songs* out on DVD in the UK now? Did it play in theatres there?

MW: Yes, it played in theatres. When we made it, I wanted it to be in the cinema and on DVD at the same time. The distributors just wouldn't do that, though I do think that's the way it's going to go, more and more. With *9 Songs*, we thought that with the music and the sex, it seemed like something people would enjoy more on DVD anyway. You know, even if a film has a short release, you get all the reviews, and then six months later the DVD comes out. For a lot of people, the film isn't going to be playing near them, and it would be nice if when they read about it, they could go get the DVD.

CS: Before you made *9 Songs*, there was *In This World*, which was a startling change of pace from *24 Hour Party People*. And that's all in the past few years. Do you consider yourself to be very prolific?

MW: It's really about working. When you're working on a film, there's a lot of very specific, concrete issues with that film, but the more you do, the more it gives you ideas for other things you'd like to do. If I took a break for a couple of years, I wouldn't have anything I wanted to make a movie about. If you keep working, it gives you energy and desire to try something else.

Michael Winterbottom: "That's How People Are"

David D'Arcy/2006

From *GreenCine*, 13 March 2006. Reprinted by permission.

Take a great work of literature and try to adapt it for the screen. You have a risk, more likely a certainty, that the film won't come close to measuring up to the original. If you bet on this expectation, you'll rarely lose. Name anything by Henry James or Ernest Hemingway or even recent fiction by Elmore Leonard, and you'll find the same problem.

Yet *Tristram Shandy; A Cock and Bull Story* by Michael Winterbottom, a loose adaptation of *The Life and Opinions of Tristram Shandy, Esq.* by Laurence Sterne (1713–68), breaks the mold, not because it's rigorous, although it is in its own way, but because it takes such freedoms with the original. Out of that approach comes a film of wit with a lightness that doesn't cheapen Laurence Sterne's novel. It opens the book up, and, one might hope, brings readers back to it.

The novel is about Tristram Shandy telling his life story and within that story is the story of Tristram's father, Walter, planning the life of his son. From this spare décor—more spare than the Masterpiece Theater opulence now branded like Burberry for the British period drama—the camera pulls back from what looks like a countercultural adaptation to Michael Winterbottom's adaptation, a backstage comedy about the making of a film about the novel.

As the director, the Winterbottom stand-in, Jeremy Northam juggles two petty egos, Steve Coogan and Rob Brydon, two actors playing themselves and their roles, who steal the show that they have helped Winterbottom and Frank Cottrell Boyce write. Coogan's ego-needs tend toward women, especially a radiant assistant (Naomie Harris) who gets aroused when the films of Fassbinder are mentioned. I did note that this was a loose adaptation. Brydon favors the undermining of anything that would give credibility to Coogan's talent or stature, and he's determined to achieve that. Think of it as an edgier version of Bob Hope and Bing Crosby in *The Road to the 18th Century*, and then add an ensemble of Brit film insiders telling in-jokes inside a country house near the set.

Just in case anyone is lost, and plenty of them probably are, Stephen Fry, as Parson Yorick, a stand-in for Sterne, reels you back in. He says matter-of-factly, "The theme of *Tristram Shandy* is quite simple. Life is chaotic, life is amorphous, and, no matter how hard you try, you can't actually put it into any kind of shape. Tristram is trying to write his life story, but it escapes him, because life is too full, too rich, to be captured by art. Tristram's father, Walter, tries to plan every aspect of Tristram's birth and childhood, but his plans go awry." That pretty much says it all.

It turns out that *Tristram Shandy*, the unfilmable novel, is not so unfilmable after all. Film can accommodate most of what this novel throws at you—the first-person voice, the voice commenting on that voice, the time shifts, the abrupt changes of subject and speaker. It helps that the mix of all these techniques is a device that we take for granted. Yet film struggles to get below the surface. Capturing the spirit of a novel does that, and getting below the surface often demands abandoning a literal rendering. Winterbottom's film is anything but that.

But make up your own mind. Read the book after you see the film.

GC: Had anyone else tried to make a film of *Tristram Shandy*?

MW: I don't think so, but I'm not sure.

GC: You've adapted two other novels, right?

MW: We did *Jude*, based on *Jude the Obscure*. And we took the story of *The Mayor of Casterbridge* and turned it into a film called *The Claim*, but it wasn't a straight adaptation. We were just using the story. For me, the thing about *Tristram Shandy* is that the book itself messes around with the story. The book tells you that it's Tristram Shandy trying to write his life story, but in fact it tells you everything but that. It deliberately keeps taking you away on any number of digressions. So, in a sense, it makes it quite easy to adapt, if you take it that that's the spirit of the book— whatever purports to be the real story is not the story you tell—then it's quite easy to find ways of telling it.

GC: Does it also free you from having to tell everything in the book?

MW: Yeah, completely. When Laurence Sterne wrote the book, he was in his forties, he was a vicar in a village in Yorkshire, and he wrote two volumes of the book, and by the end of the first two volumes, Tristram Shandy hasn't even been born. He tried to get them published, but no one would publish them, so he paid to get them published himself. When it came out, it was a huge success. The very nature of what he's doing is that he says he's telling the story, but he deliberately avoids telling the story, and he goes out on endless digressions. It's in the very nature of how he writes that, in order to make a screenplay of it, you don't want to do a literal version of the book. What was nice is that when we finished the film, we had a lot of help from a trust that runs a museum in the house where he lived, in this village. We showed the film in the village hall on a digital projector. A lot of people from the village came, but also *Tristram Shandy* experts from England and from Europe and Canada. They all loved it, because I think that if you liked the book, you wouldn't want a literal adaptation. It goes against the spirit of the book. The spirit of the book is to mess around and have fun, be anarchic, deliberately confound expectations. So whereas perhaps Dickens experts or Austen experts or Hardy experts would want it to be the book, the Sterne experts would also be very happy to find things that weren't in the book.

GC: The film seems to have taken that stop-and-start interrupted discontinuity as the spirit of the book. But making a film itself is a structural set of digressions, with the hurry-up-and-wait syndrome as actors and director wait until the lighting and everything else is in place. Idleness begets storytelling (which doesn't have to be focused on any particular subject) and storytelling begets discussion of the stories told. It's part of *The Arabian Nights* as much as it is part of *Tristram Shandy*.

MW: Yeah—well, the last scene of the film is pretty much the last scene of the book. In the book you read for hundreds of pages and then he asks, "What is this all about?—it's a cock and bull story." And it stops, and that's it. I think generally in films I try to avoid stories that have a journey, and they have an arc, and characters learn something, and they have a traditional dramatic shape, because that seems to be so the opposite of life. In life, it's all random, everything happens when you least expect, things stop and start. People on the whole don't learn. Life isn't about starting out innocent and ending up wise, learning these lessons. You spend a lot of time repeating the same mistakes over and over again. The enjoyable thing about the book is that it forgives all those flaws, all those idiocies. It forgives them. So I hope that the film has the same tone of warmth and affection—that no matter how stupidly Steve behaves, that's how people are. But you don't have to condemn them for it.

GC: Can you think of a contemporary novel that gives a comparable perspective, that is the *Tristram Shandy* of its time?

MW: When Sterne is writing, it's the early stages of novel-writing, and novel-writing then is very much playing with how to write the story. You've got lots of first-person narration, you've got Fielding, you've got all sorts of epistolary novels. In a way, that was the mainstream of the novel at the time. It wasn't a self-conscious literary device. People were saying, We've got the form to tell stories, what are the ways of doing it? But I think of something like Dave Eggers's book, *A Heartbreaking Work of Staggering Genius*. There are a lot of the same devices there. And he equally has a very warm story of family affection.

GC: Why did you decide to make your film about the making of a movie?

MW: Because so much of the book is about writing the book. It's pretty deadly to watch a film where a lot of people are spending a lot of time writing. The reason he used that in the book is so he can mess around with what he's actually writing, so that he talks a lot about the problems of writing so he can play with the narration. It seemed to me that it was the best parallel, the best equivalent. And also, there was this modern section, where you have a character called Steve Coogan and a character called Rob Brydon, and you're with the people in the cast and crew. I have to say that, although I've done period films, I find them quite tricky. It's not my most comfortable genre. I liked the fact that there was the possibility of the modern section as well. For me it was a big relief—it was a relief for Steve and Rob, too—to shoot the period stuff first, and then step outside it.

GC: How *did* you shoot? Did you shoot this in sequence? Does the fragmented process of making any film lend itself to the spirit of the book?

MW: I do try to shoot in sequence as much as possible. If you keep it simple, it generally does help. It is fragmented. In the perfect world of acting, you obviously want to know exactly what's in the next scene, you want to know what your emotional moment is, what the transition is from this scene to the next. That works in a crafted kind of story, but personally I prefer more the idea that actors just respond to that moment, so when we filmed, we'd film in one take—the whole scene—and then we'd do it again, and again. Each time they do it, they can try different things, they can say different things, they can react in different ways. It's not continuity that they have to repeat. And I like the fact that they don't have to do the scene one way instead of another. This way it's fresh. It corresponds more to how people behave. People don't behave in a continuous way. People change. One moment you're dealing with one thing. The next moment you're dealing with another. So you don't have to be consistent.

GC: Did you require the cast to read the novel?

MW: We sent the book to Steve and Rob, but we had no expectations that they would read it, and they didn't read it.

GC: Did that matter?

MW: I kind of think that it's not relevant either way. Would they be better if they'd read it? I think definitely not. I do think Naomie Harris read the book. So I didn't have a thing that I said, you mustn't read the book. But I don't think it's relevant. It's not about doing homework. It's more about working with Steve and Rob about how to find things to do in the film, as opposed to "Is this in the book?" or "What was the character's motivation?" We couldn't deal with the characters this way. The book is a game or a play. It doesn't really give you background material.

GC: Did you rehearse at all? Was there any point to rehearsing?

MW: I'm not a big fan of rehearsing. Steve and Rob were cast in this before we started writing, so we talked to them about stuff when we were writing. They would suggest things, and then we would go away and write bits and pieces. They were discussions rather than rehearsals. Steve would suggest a detail that we would then spend time on, like the heel of a shoe, and then we would come back to him with what we'd written.

GC: This is hardly the prototype for screen adaptations of novels. Often the example that's given of the best adaptation of a novel, obviously along more conventional lines, is *Great Expectations*, which David Lean made in 1946. Clearly, *Tristram Shandy* is a very different kind of book and film. But if you did have an ideal example of an adaptation, what would it be?

MW: Good question. [Hesitates] *The Big Sleep* is a pretty good film. I don't think that when you watch a film you really think about that. I'm sure that there are quite a lot, but not because they're your favorite novels. In the end, you watch the film and you enjoy the film, whether it's based on a book or not. It doesn't really matter—great book, great film—because I don't think there's that much connection in the end. I think you can make great films out of great books, but not because they are great books. It just happens by chance. I don't think you choose a great book because it's going to make a great film. It's two separate things.

GC: What about the notion that the lesser the book, the better the chance you have to make it into a good film?

MW: It's true in the sense that, if you feel freer in relation to the book, maybe that's good. Because if you're putting stuff into the film because it's in the book, that's not a good enough reason. There's a million things that go into making a film—whether you get it from a book, or from your head, or from a magazine article. The source material is just one part. The main story is Tristram trying to tell the story of his life, and the main story within that is Walter, his father, trying to plan his childhood. Now that's the core of the book, and then we had a difference of opinion, the writer and myself, about the direction the film should take, because I thought it should have a modern side to it, and he didn't. He was very keen to have a lot more of Uncle Toby and Widow Wadman. A lot of the talk about the script in the film came from discussions we had. So we extracted the script from scenes in the book. The elements in the script that are taken from the book are very close to the book, and that leaves you with questions about how to arrange the material. Very early on, it was clear that, although there are masses of material in the book, [much of] it wasn't going to go into the film, so it became very, very much about characters trying to get to the birth, or trying to get to each other, and that became the heart for us. And then it became how to extend ideas that were in the book, themes that were in the book, into the modern sections. So the idea was that Steve was playing Steve in the film, and Tristram and Walter, but they were all variations on the same character. So you could play around with some of the same emotions and ideas there as well.

GC: Young people, as you know, don't read much, and they don't read eighteenth century classics, so this might just become the *Tristram Shandy* of their generation. How do you feel about that? Does it give you a greater sense of responsibility?

MW: I don't think that many people were aware of *Tristram Shandy* anyway, so . . .

GC: So it's better than nothing?

MW: One thing that I've said is that we worked quite closely with the Shandy Trust, and their curator read the script, and talked to us about the book and so on, and those who have read the book, and know the book, whose lives are entangled with the book, seem genuinely happy about the version we made and about our approach to it. It's not the kind of book where, if it's changed from the original, it's confusing or distorting. It's more that, if you like the book, you would like the idea of someone messing around with it, and I think we're open that we're messing around with it. We're not saying this is the book. We're messing around with the book.

GC: Did Sterne write multiple versions of the novel?

MW: He wrote two volumes and then he extended beyond it. He became a celebrity. He became famous and very successful. I don't know whether he planned to write other volumes or how many volumes he planned. He probably didn't have a shape to the novel. He just kind of kept writing. Then, since he was a vicar, he made sermons, and he issued the sermons under the title, "The Sermons of Yorick," so he was playing around with the idea of him being a character in the book. He played with exactly the same things that we were playing with, really.

GC: What did you find out about the book from Sterne specialists, or about the specialists themselves?

MW: Obviously the book is so open to experiments in structure and form that this project is very much about things that have happened between now and then. And when you go to the village where he wrote the book, and you go to his house, there is an amazing continuity. The houses are still the houses that people live in, the place is very much the place it was when Sterne was writing. The concerns of the novel— planning the birth of your baby, planning for his education, of course these are the same things that people are worried about now. The people whom we met were all big enthusiasts. I think Sterne was about forty-five when he wrote the book. He became rich from it and he spent a lot of time in London. Sterne died of TB about six years or seven after that, so he had a short period of fame. He fell in love with a younger woman. He really lived the celebrity life, transformed from this parson. He had his portrait commissioned. It was very much like what life is like for Steve now, enjoying the benefits of celebrity.

GC: And there is always the element of self-parody with Sterne, looking at this life for the joke that it is.

MW: It's a joke because he's trying to be funny. I'm not sure that Sterne ever intended to write the whole book. He only wrote two volumes, and then carried on. So there's a lack of pattern in the whole book, very deliberate, but partly a consequence of how it was written.

GC: There's a Dogme look to your film, a lot of continuous shooting, continuous performance. Is the Dogme movement important to you?

MW: No. I think the idea of Dogme is. I was on the jury in Cannes when the first two Dogme films came out. I think the idea of Dogme was a good publicity stunt, but it's kind of bullshit for filmmakers. If you have to have rules and you have to make films the same way, that's bullshit. But obviously they knew that as well. They did it as a publicity stunt. So I admire them for the way they handled that sort of stuff, and generated a lot of interest around it. And *Breaking the Waves* was a great film, but it was pre-Dogme. I like to work in similar ways. I like hand-held, I like to work with available light, if possible. I like to shoot whole scenes. There obviously are a lot of connections. To me, when you're making a film, it's hard enough that you have to make the best version of that film. The idea that you have a book of rules that requires you to do something is obviously bullshit. If you're making a film, the simpler you make it, the better, the more fun it is. If you can make it with two people in the crew, that's nice. If you have a bigger crew, that's just more stuff going on. I always try to make it as simple as possible.

GC: After seeing the film in Toronto, a studio executive who also liked it asked me if the film was too smart to make any money. I told him I hoped not.

MW: I'd rather make a film that I like and people don't watch, than a film that I don't like and other people do watch.

In Praise of Folly: An Interview with Michael Winterbottom

Richard Porton/2006

From *Cineaste* 31, no. 2 (Spring 2006): 28–31. Reprinted by permission.

During his whirlwind career as a director, Michael Winterbottom has emerged as something of a chameleon. Befuddling auteurists who reduce directors' careers to a constricting set of themes and stylistic choices, Winterbottom's films include sober adaptations of Thomas Hardy, forays into political cinema such as *Welcome to Sarajevo* and *In This World*, an earnest jab at dystopian science fiction—*Code 46*—and *9 Songs*, a curious amalgam of hard-core sex and rock-concert film. Despite this dizzying eclecticism, Winterbottom's recent films—*9 Songs*, *24 Hour Party People* (a faux biopic of the British rock impresario Tony Wilson), and his most recent work, *Tristram Shandy: A Cock and Bull Story*, all favor a low-budget, stripped-down esthetic which imbues even the most over-the-top antics with a documentary immediacy.

Blessed with a puckish sense of humor, Winterbottom was no doubt attracted to Laurence Sterne's eccentric eighteenth-century novel, *The Life and Opinions of Tristram Shandy, Gentleman*, by dint of its sheer unfilmability. While Winterbottom's film is a brilliant comic jape as well as a thoroughly valid, and appropriately irreverent reinterpretation of *Tristram Shandy*, early reviews that identify Sterne's comic masterpiece as a mere predecessor of modernist and postmodernist fiction are a bit off the mark. While contemporary experiments in metafiction often deliquesce into solipsism or cynicism, Sterne's robust eighteenth-century humanism can be viewed as an antidote to modern paeans to alienation. Sterne's engagement with the empiricism of Locke and Hume inspired him to consider the quandary of the isolated individual—supposedly doomed to only comprehend reality through sensory experience.

97

Yet, as an antinomian clergyman who also derived sustenance from the Renaissance humanism of Rabelais and Erasmus, Sterne's radical skepticism and playful subversion of linguistic propriety and linear narrative is inextricable from a celebration of creative fecundity and the power of literature to transcend the prison of the self.

Winterbottom intuitively responds to Sterne's celebration of the eighteenth-century concept of *discordia concors*—the notion of "harmony through discord"—that provides the impetus for the anarchic vignettes in both the film and novel. In a narrative where Tristram, the supposed protagonist, is not even born until hundreds of pages have elapsed, elaborate digressions become focal points instead of distractions. Eschewing the convoluted discussions of religion, philosophy, and warfare that slow down the modern reader of Sterne, Winterbottom instead interweaves some of the key incidents from the novel with a framing story in which the filming of *Tristram Shandy: A Cock and Bull Story* itself becomes a fictional construct—and a fun-house mirror reflection of the travails and pleasures of shooting a movie. This device allows a subtle alternation between picaresque farce (and a fairly earnest effort to be true to the nuances of the period) and a manically comic version of the film à clef genre that includes such illustrious precursors as *8½*, *Contempt*, and *Day for Night*. Paradoxically enough, a healthy disrespect (mingled with affection) for Sterne's novel is perfectly in keeping with the spirit of *Tristram Shandy* and a running joke throughout the film emphasizes the fact that almost none of the actors have actually managed the long slog through the nearly seven-hundred-page text.

In a maneuver that proved both commercially sound and loyal to Sterne's gentle humor, Winterbottom cast a host of British comedians blessed with the ability to improvise as both themselves and key protagonists of this quintessential shaggy dog story. As Tristram Shandy, his own pedantic father Walter, and a somewhat cartoonish version of himself, Steve Coogan (known in England as the star of several sitcoms featuring his beloved alter ego, obnoxiously narcissistic TV host Alan Partridge) embodies both the playfulness and self-denigration that is at the heart of the film's modern reinvention of Sterne's benign lunacy. Coogan's comic nemesis—as well as Sterne's hapless Uncle Toby—is played by Rob Brydon, a comedian little known in the States but famous for voice-overs and television work in Britain. Given Sterne's famous preoccupation with sundry varieties of male inadequacy (Toby's evocation of a groin wound suffered at the Battle of Namur is one of the book's set pieces), the contrapuntal banter improvised by Brydon and Coogan effortlessly arrives at modern, show-business equivalents of the Shandean brand of male neurosis. Coogan frets about his height and billing, finding time to rib second banana Brydon about his yellowing teeth. Brydon, a good-natured foil, gamely labels his incisors akin to jaundiced shades of "Barley Meadow" and "Tuscan Sunset" while proclaiming that, "If you think your teeth are too good, you get bogged down in the leading-men category."

Winterbotttom's generosity towards his self-absorbed characters takes a huge cue from Uncle Toby's famous propensity to straddle his hobbyhorse while reminiscing about his youthful glory on the battlefield during the War of the Spanish Succession. All of the characters are celebrated, not admonished, for their determination to ride disparate hobbyhorses with a combination of vigor and dyspepsia. Cinema, and by implication life, is conceived of as a convivial convergence of half-crazed obsessives. To wit, Walter Shandy's monomaniacal interest in eighteenth-century obstetrics is easily translated into Coogan's New Agey immersion in childrearing. (Kelly Macdonald plays his stoic girlfriend.) In a similar vein, Coogan flirts shamelessly with Jenny (Naomie Harris), a pretty production assistant—whose "hobbyhorse" consists of a charming tendency to flaunt her enthusiasm for movies (particularly obscure Fassbinder films) at inappropriate times. The equanimity with which the film views its characters' diverse quirks perhaps suggests that Sterne's tolerance for all varieties of human folly can be seen as a premodern equivalent of Jean Renoir's credo in *Rules of the Game*— "Everyone has their reasons."

Tristram Shandy: A Cock and Bull Story's impish disregard for the niceties of realism (the de facto esthetic of contemporary British cinema) seems to have scared the film's initial investors; the fact that funding came through for the project at only the last minute aptly complements the project's jubilant ad hoc esthetic. In the following interview, conducted at the time of the film's North American premiere at the 2005 New York Film Festival, Winterbottom discusses with detached aplomb financial woes, his longstanding interest in literary adaptation, and his fondness for Coogan and Brydon. Even his tendency to nonchalantly mumble his responses seemed in keeping with the studied casualness that makes his "cock and bull story" such an unexpected delight.

Cineaste: Since you directed two well-received adaptations of Hardy novels, I suppose you've given some thought to assumptions that films should be faithful to their sources. These notions, of course, go out the window with an adaptation of *Tristram Shandy*; the very idea of faithfulness would be absurd in relationship to Sterne's novel. What you've done, however, is very faithful to the spirit of the novel.

Michael Winterbottom: Although I don't think it actually matters if it's faithful to the novel, the idea was to do something that was faithful to the spirit of *Tristram Shandy*. I had already done a film called *24 Hour Party People*, which, although obviously about a much different subject, was in slightly the same spirit. We shot the film in the village hall in the same town where Sterne had written the book. There's a trust that looks after his papers and tries to promote work in a similar spirit and the town was full of *Tristram Shandy* experts. There are very few *Tristram Shandy* fans, but if you are one you probably don't want a film to be a literal transcription of the book. So it was great. The fans were very happy that it takes the book as a starting point and then goes off in a totally different direction.

Cineaste: From what I've read, the Sterne scholars are very happy with the film.

Winterbottom: Yes, it was good; we had a successful first screening with many of them in attendance. Of course, the primary aim was to make a film and not to please scholars.

Cineaste: Is it true that the origins of this project began some years ago with you and Frank Cottrell Boyce discussing the outline of a script?

Winterbottom: Yeah, we sort of talked about it on and off for a while during a ten-year period—not writing the script but just talking about the idea of doing it. We also talked about *Tristram Shandy* when we were doing *24 Hour Party People*. In the end, we thought, "Why not have a go at the book?" And, having worked with Steve [Coogan] on *24 Hour Party People* and having talked about the narrative devices in the film, with him as the narrator and all of the playfulness and stupidity of his character, I was eager to find something to work on with him again.

Cineaste: And you thought from the outset that it was a good idea to cast primarily comic actors in the main roles?

Winterbottom: Yeah, the book is a comic novel. Also, I had worked with Steve and a little bit with Rob before. They bring the ability to project some aspects of themselves into their characters. That generation of British comedians, who came up through stand-up and improvisation, often generate their own material. They're also thinking about how they can embellish their characters or even write their own material. When you give a script to someone like Steve—or in fact to most of the people in the film—they're very relaxed about trying things out. It's a very organic approach to fleshing out the script.

Cineaste: So the process of working on the film was obviously much looser than working on a film like *Jude*.

Winterbottom: Yeah, definitely. The period sections within *Tristram* are quite close to the book. There isn't much improvisation there, but even in those sequences, since the tone of the book is quite silly, you feel that you can play around and don't feel you have to be obsessed with authenticity. *Jude* was a book I loved as a teenager; it was one of my favorite books. Although I wanted to be faithful to that book, I don't find Hardy as pessimistic or fatalistic a writer as some people think. He's quite radical in what he says about society and class. It's very hard when making an adaptation of a period novel, however, to make it feel as fresh as it would have been to people at the time while still retaining a sense of the specific historical context. It's an impossible balance. With *Tristram Shandy*, we've tried to keep the silliness while creating characters that also live in their own fictional world.

Cineaste: I suppose the obvious question involves how much of the script is the result of the actors' own input—particularly Coogan and Brydon.

Winterbottom: Steve was given the script first. So he helped to flesh out his role at an early stage. The idea was to have Steve and Rob on set where they could create situations and feel free to change and revise the script. The very first scene and the last one were completely made up on the set as the result of saying, "Let's just see what happens." Within other scenes, it varies. The idea is that, if anyone has anything to contribute, we should try and encourage them. The great thing about Rob and Steve—as well as Dylan Moran and David Walliams—is that they come from a tradition where they're used to creating their characters. So it's great to work with them because they always have something new to try out. There's always more going on in the scene than you originally planned.

Cineaste: Is Jeremy Northam, in the role of the director, providing some version or parody of you? In some respects, the project became a sort of film à clef.

Winterbottom: I don't know if that was the intention, but it does seem that he's slightly mimicking my behavior at times. Since we were on a film set making a film partially about a film set, the idea was that it was easier to borrow certain aspects of the actual shoot and incorporate these into the script. It's not that it was important for aspects of the film to be true; it was just easier to borrow things that were happening rather than generating all sorts of fictional events. So the discussion in the film about whether to include the Widow Wadman actually mirrored some actual discussions we'd had at an earlier point.

Cineaste: And your producer has remarked that many of the observations of investors in *Tristram Shandy* (e.g., "Don't hold us ransom") actually recall incidents that occurred on various films you've worked on.

Winterbottom: Yeah, on *Tristram* we were having terrible financial problems off set and what happens in the film is actually a much milder version of these conflicts. The original people who agreed to finance it backed out before shooting began. So it was all very stressful and down to the wire.

Cineaste: In addition, Gillian Anderson's speedy acceptance of the part of the Widow Wadman probably can be viewed as mocking the much more arduous process of wooing actors to appear in a film.

Winterbottom: Yes, it was deliberately absurd—as far away from the truth as possible. Although it was actually quite simple to convince Gillian, the idea was to make the situation comic by just calling her up and having her accept immediately without any elaborate negotiations.

Cineaste: Were you inspired by other films that dealt with the filmmaking process? You obviously use the Nina Rota music from *8½* and there are many other prototypes such as *Day for Night*.

Winterbottom: There are actually quite a lot of good films dealing with filmmaking. All the music in the film is from other films—not only *8½* but also *The Draughtsman's Contract* and *Smiles of a Summer Night*. You're aware of what music works, but also of the collections, and it's quite fun to play around with that sort of thing. Handel is also appropriate for the period. The original idea wasn't to make a film about filmmaking. We started with *Tristram Shandy* and the idea was that filmmaking was analogous to Sterne's preoccupation with writing and playfulness. We then extended that to more specific concerns with babies and the chaos of life. We just wanted to have an equivalent to all of the distractions in life that move you away from your core concerns.

Cineaste: *Tristram Shandy* is a novel about process and digressions. And you have found cinematic equivalents to some of his literary jokes, such as the use of a blank screen instead of a blank page.

Winterbottom: Yeah, the whole modern-day plot is really a digression, although there are actually much longer digressions in the novel. Sterne has digressions that go on for a hundred pages. It was also very easy to tweak the material to suit Steve; he's very good at portraying a version of himself.

Cineaste: And the idea of mock autobiography is also very true to Sterne and the period.

Winterbottom: Like in *Tristram Shandy* itself, there's the fact that Sterne was a vicar and Yorick is a vicar character and we have an account in the novel of the sins of Yorick. So there's sort of a bridge there between fiction and real life.

Cineaste: Since Steve Coogan, like his character in the film, has also found himself discussed in the tabloids at times, perhaps it's an opportunity for him to parody himself.

Winterbottom: Yeah, although I'm not sure if parody is the best word. He's exaggerated certain aspects of himself. But, in the end, I hope you see the character as human and not at all grotesque. It's not that he's a terrible person; it's just that we have someone running around worried about details, worried about unimportant things, and we should conclude, "Isn't that what everyone does?"

Cineaste: Of course, the idea that this is what everyone does goes back to Sterne's preoccupation with Uncle Toby on his hobbyhorse. When we look with detachment at all of these people on the movie set on their own hobbyhorses, it becomes rather endearing.

Winterbottom: Exactly, just as the characters in *Tristram Shandy* are endearing. Even the most irritating obsessions, such as with Steve's obsession with his heels in the film (which was Steve's idea, actually), can be seen as sort of endearing. In the end—although, yes, it's about vanity and his obsession with status—you can say that actors do actually worry about these details and films are, in the end, just a collection of details. Everyone has to worry about their details and they all eventually coalesce and make sense.

Cineaste: Even the production assistant on the film, whose role in the filmmaking is quite minor, brings her own obsession with movies to the set. Is this a phenomenon you've noticed on various films?

Winterbottom: I don't think there's much of a connection between your seniority and your enthusiasm for your role in the film. It's quite rare, though, that you get someone who's that committed to the film-making process. Again, we're not really satirizing her obsessions but saying that it's great that she's so passionate. We're just looking at all of the characters' hobbyhorses and, to a certain extent, their weaknesses. But we're also implying that their weaknesses can be their strengths.

Cineaste: Since you like a certain verisimilitude on your films (e.g., shooting at the actual site of Factory Records in *24 Hour Party People*), was it important for you to shoot at the actual Shandy Hall?

Winterbottom: Yeah, obviously if you're shooting period material, you want to get it right—and there are a lot of houses from that period available. But, to a certain extent, there were differences between the modern sequences and what actually ensued on set—the characters in the film stay in a hotel that's much grander than the one we stayed in. But we tried to make the two parts of the film quite visually similar—a lot of hand-held material and use of natural light.

Cineaste: To a certain extent, with both *9 Songs* and this film, you're moving towards a more stripped-down esthetic.

Winterbottom: Yeah, the idea now is to keep things as simple as possible. Although, with *Tristram*, you couldn't possibly have a shoot that was as simple as *9 Songs* or *Wonderland* since the period stuff demanded you have a bigger cast with more elements to choreograph and, ultimately, a bigger crew.

Cineaste: I also read that you worked closely with Patrick Wildgust, the curator of Shandy Hall.

Winterbottom: We visited him before we started writing the script. He was very sweet and enthusiastic and runs Shandy Hall as a sort of trust. He read the script and offered Shandy Hall for the first screening of the film. I think Patrick would have preferred to have played himself in the film. But we thought that Stephen Fry would ultimately bring more to the part. And since Stephen Fry was also playing Yorick, we thought that the two roles would overlap quite nicely in the end with the scene featuring the cock and bull.

Cineaste: I suppose that's a scene you must have envisioned quite early on.

Winterbottom: Yeah, it's just that we were struggling to figure out how to end a film based on a book that's so open-ended—and, in a sense, has no ending. The ending of the book is so arbitrary and so abrupt—bang, it's over!—that we thought perhaps our best solution was to get back into the book at that point—and then it's Laurence Sterne's fault, not our fault. Actually, outside of America, this film is simply titled *A Cock and Bull Story*, not *Tristram Shandy: A Cock and Bull Story*. That's to emphasize that, in the end, it's not to be taken too seriously. Even though we might seem to be striving for some sort of seriousness or some kind of overarching design, we wanted to make the point that it's deliberately a shaggy dog story.

Cineaste: *Tristram Shandy* is sort of the grandfather of shaggy dog stories—something that's recognized in Steve Coogan's line that it was a "postmodernist novel before there was even modernism."

Winterbottom: Yes, the playfulness is quite modern—and that's how the novel started, didn't it?—with Fielding and Defoe messing around with narration. But, even if the playfulness is quite modern, some of the digressions Sterne goes into aren't very modern. We'd be testing an audience's patience if we retained a lot of that. That's why we kept returning to the relationship between the father and son; the father's obsession with every aspect of his wife's labor and child's education brings to mind some very modern obsessions. This is mirrored of course in the modern scenes and Steve's preoccupation with his child. We wanted to see if we could achieve a structure that seemed completely chaotic but still made sense.

Michael Winterbottom's Road Movie

David D'Arcy/2006

From *GreenCine*, 6 July 2006. Reprinted by permission.

In February, I thought that *The Road to Guantánamo* was one of the high points of the Berlin International Film Festival, where it made its world premiere. After seeing the film again recently, just before its release in the U.S. this past weekend, I still feel that way. The story is of four young men of Pakistani origin traveling from the English Midlands to Pakistan, then venturing for vaguely charitable reasons into Afghanistan, where three are caught up in the town of Kunduz as the Taliban surrender to the Northern Alliance. They are taken prisoner with everyone else that the Northern Alliance rounds up, and eventually sent to Guantánamo, where they are subjected to abusive interrogations that the U.S. says fall short of torture. (Ask the recent suicides whether they thought it was torture.)

The film operates mostly as a dramatic recreation of these events, culminating with the release of the Tipton Three from their prison in Cuba when documents showed clearly that none of them had been present at Al Qaeda meetings before 9/11 that they were accused of attending. (A fourth friend was lost on the Afghan-Pakistani border, and has never been heard from since.) In a film that could have been either a lecture or a newsreel, there's a sensitivity to character and context here, a gritty nose-to-the-ground tactility that directors Michael Winterbottom and Mat Whitecross achieved with a shoestring crew. It's the chronicle of a miscarriage of justice—if justice really is the word that should be used— a humanizing look under the hood, if you'll permit that awful turn of phrase. You wonder, if these three men were innocent, how many more of the prisoners there might be just as innocent. Perhaps we could even find out—if the U.S. government would just show that the "enemy combatants" caged there were really terrorists. It would only involve bringing them before a court and allowing lawyers for the men to evaluate the evidence.

In the frenzy of press coverage that spiked in Berlin and has surged again with the film's release, two criticisms of *The Road to Guantánamo* recur.

One charge is that the film is one-sided, which I assume presupposes the criticism that the film does not conform to the Fox News "fair and balanced" approach to reporting. (What ever happened to fair and accurate, the real standard?) It is a dramatic feature film, after all, but in today's situation, in which gaps in reporting are indeed filled by films, books, blogs, talk shows, and television programs, we can also view and evaluate this film as a work of journalism. It's not a systematic study of Guantánamo, but rather, the story of the three men, corroborated by sworn testimony from the three of them to their lawyer. We hear the young men's stories, in re-creation and in testimony from Asif Iqbal, Shafiq Rasul, and Ruhel Ahmed. We also hear interrogators repeat over and over that the three were in Pakistan planning terrorist attacks, offering as proof the photos in which the men are alleged to appear. In the face of that "evidence," the men repeat that they were in England at that time. It could have been checked easily enough, in less than a week. When it finally is checked, after two years, the men are released. What a way to run a war.

You can find a certain kind of balance in Winterbottom's film in the tension between men who proclaim their innocence (except for Asif's confession after a torture session) and men assigned to get information out of them, even if that means coercing a false confession out of a man who's been shackled into a squatting position. Perhaps the balance that critics demand could have been enhanced by cutting to shots of the burning World Trade Center, the reason for the War on Terror. Would those shots of New York under siege have made the three detainees any less innocent?

The other criticism is that we really don't know if the three men went into Afghanistan to help suffering Muslims there, as they say they did. Statements by anyone trying to avoid prison or torture are best viewed with skepticism. They are also best verified, as are any charges brought against them. Ultimately, after insisting that the three men were in Pakistan attending Al Qaeda rallies before 9/11, the U.S. and the U.K. could substantiate nothing against the men, and they were set free. The U.S. position still seems to be that the detainees at Guantánamo were (and are) "bad men," some of "the worst," George W. Bush said, because they were foreigners in Afghanistan and, ergo, Al Qaeda. With "intelligence" like that, you can't be too encouraged, and torture isn't going to make that "intelligence" any more reliable. If, as an investigation, *The Road to Guantánamo* is deficient, and I don't think it is, the solution is more investigation. The U.S., with all its resources, couldn't find implicating evidence. Good luck to the enterprising journalists (critical of the film, as many are) who are willing to take their shots. Don't hold your breath.

The Road to Guantánamo really follows two roads. The main narrative takes us through a road trip, into a war (with as much confusing "fog" as any war), and then into a prison saga in which jailers try to "break" men in cages, three innocent men. The three men who were never charged travel toward Cuba by way of a trip to Pakistan, then to Afghanistan, then in stifling cargo containers with no air, water, or food (Camp X-Ray seems like Canyon Ranch, compared to that experience), then to a C-130 in which they're shackled to the walls for what must have been an endless ride, and then to the cages in which they are blindfolded and subjected to what sure seems like torture, regardless of the excuses that are subsidized with your tax dollars. As the detainees' lawyer Joseph Margulies explains in his valuable book, *Guantánamo and the Abuse of Presidential Power*, prisoners are brought to despair to get them to talk—not for the purpose of providing information that will convict them and prove that the government was correct to round them up and torture them, but for the purpose of pre-empting another attack on the U.S., or so we're told.

Besides the prisoners' road to, and eventually, from Guantánamo, there's the road that the U.S. took to get there, the odyssey of a government caught sleeping (that had shifted anti-terrorism resources under John Ashcroft from the hunt for bin Laden to the hunt for child pornography). Embarrassed, the government solution has been blunt overkill, justifying a foreign invasion on evidence as slim as the evidence against the Tipton Three, and condoning "legitimate interrogation techniques" as anything that falls short of organ failure. A U.S. general referred officially to the recent suicides as "asymmetric warfare."

This second road is the road less-scrutinized in this film, the road taken away from accountability and toward the official legitimizing of what we used to call "cruel and unusual punishment." Like any narrative that is constrained by logistics and form (and the demands of entertainment) to assemble its elements selectively, this one asks you to fill in the blanks, to draw conclusions based on the intelligence you have.

The Road to Guantánamo is a gripping drama that's as exciting as anything on the screen right now. It's the story of three prisoners and how they got there, by no means the definitive word on the prison and the policy that condones torture there. How could it be, with events unfolding right now, and prisoners petitioning the U.S. for compensation, and a secret prison at Bagram Air Base in Afghanistan that seems to be designated as the new Guantánamo? Stay tuned.

Michael Winterbottom does manage to get in a dig or two that he must have enjoyed. The "Guantánamo" that was reconstructed for the film was built in Iran, the "axis of evil" state, where much of the film was shot. Filming this exposé (destined for a U.S. public, among others) in Iran must have been a bit like Hugo Chávez sending free oil to Americans who couldn't afford the rising corporate fuel prices last winter.

I spoke to Michael Winterbottom when he was in New York for the film's U.S. release.

Q: There's a lot of talk about this film filling in gaps of information that the press hasn't covered. It's been a constant theme. How do you view that? There was a lot of reporting about these three young men in the British press, quite a lot, although you might argue that newspaper articles don't have the impact of a single feature film. Did press reports help you, or did you end up having to do most of the research for this story yourself?

A: We're telling the story of just these three individuals. It's very specific. It's not a film about a general situation. The research was that Mat Whitecross, the other director, spent a month living in with them, so we have hundreds of hours of tapes with them. They'd also done a deposition with Gareth Pierce, their lawyer, so in a sense the research for this film was very specific. The reason we made this film was that we had read the story of these guys in the press. But when we were searching the archive for material for the film, the news archive, it was interesting to go back to the beginning of Guantánamo and see the way it was reported then. It was a huge story, and you could see from the way the journalists were reporting it that they couldn't quite get their heads around it themselves. "Hang on, America's got this prison in Cuba, these people are going to be covered by American law or by international law, they aren't treated as prisoners of war?" Those first images of all the guys in the orange jump suits being held in Camp X-Ray were very powerful. It's not that the press hasn't done its job. There are individual journalists who have tried to keep writing about it. The *Observer*, for instance, and the TV news covered it. But what happens is that, no matter what you think of Guantánamo, after two years it's not a story anymore. It's very hard to keep saying, "Look, it's still here." So it just seemed that, if we made the film, it would be one other way of reminding people that Guantánamo is still there. Also, if you see three individuals—that's part of the reason I wanted them to be in the film—and you hear their story, it gives you a different perspective on Guantánamo, because so much of the imagery, so much of the way the situation was handled by the American authorities was to make them anonymous. They didn't release the names, they didn't tell you very much about them. They all looked the same, all were kept so far away that it was always very distant. It was always this very strange group of people about whom we were always told that they were the worst of the worst, the most dangerous terrorists in the world, who are such a big threat that we have to have them like this. Our idea was that, if for an hour and a half in the cinema you're watching three individuals and what happened to them, that will give you an extra layer of understanding.

Q: There's a genre in American film, dramatic feature and documentary, of the wronged individual or individuals, the victims of miscarriages of justice railroaded, as we would say, into prison. I'm thinking of *I Am a Fugitive from a Chain Gang* or *The Thin Blue Line* or the recent *Trials of Darryl Hunt*, which shows how an innocent man can be kept in prison for years after there's overwhelming evidence of his innocence. There are also comedies in this vein, like *Sullivan's Travels* by Preston Sturges, in which a millionaire posing as a homeless man in a research project for a film is arrested, convicted, and jailed. Were you thinking of this genre at all when you decided to make a feature film about the Tipton Three?

A: No, to be honest. The film is split into three parts. There's a road movie, there's a war movie, and there's a prison movie. What we're doing is very simply telling their story—to try and avoid the normal genre conventions, to try and avoid the fictional dramatic devices you would normally use to try to make a story interesting. The story in the film is told to you by the three guys, and the re-creations simply reenact things that they are telling us. I was trying to avoid it being dramatic, in a way, and certainly trying to avoid it being fictional, trying to avoid characters, even. This is also not a film that is about wronged individuals. I wouldn't want people to leave the cinema thinking, "These guys were so unlucky. These are the three innocent ones, and everyone else there was guilty." I certainly don't want people to think that these guys were unlucky to have a bunch of guards who went crazy and tortured them. What we're trying to show is that this is the routine of the system. This is not a film about the individual isolated example which is different to the general. Shafiq, Ruhel, and Asif, in a way, had a very easy time there. What you see happening in *Guantánamo* is just the routine of the system, the routine of interrogation. So things like stress positions, short shacklings, strobe lights, loud music, the isolation—all these things are part of what the system of Guantánamo does, which the system in Guantánamo feels is acceptable. This is just what goes on routinely in Guantánamo, and hopefully, people, when they watch the film, will think that this shouldn't happen. But the [Bush] administration thinks it should be like that, and it's set up so these things do happen.

Q: Had you thought of making a straight documentary about this?

A: It could have been. It seems to me that this isn't a drama or documentary, because we aren't trying to dramatize this. It could have been them talking and telling their story, although you'd have to be incredibly fluent storytellers to hold people's attention. But it seemed to me also that when you get to the point where you're in Guantánamo, or Kabul, or Karachi, then you see what Kabul is like, you see Karachi, you see what Guantánamo looks like physically, that gives you a lot of extra information in a simple quick way. It's a more effective, shorter way of trying to tell people what Guantánamo looks like. You just build it, rather than have someone describe it to you.

Q: How much did you rely on information besides what you got from the three young men who were incarcerated and their lawyer? Did you talk to interrogators? Did you get anything from "the other side"?

A: The reason for the shape of the film, to be clear, is that this is them telling their story. They never were brought to court, they never had a chance to tell their story, so this is them telling their story. We didn't do a huge amount of cross-checking their story, but then there's not that many areas that you can cross-check. From all the testimony by former detainees, from people with opinions like Clive Stafford-Smith, their lawyer, who represents detainees, and from administration documents, these are routine techniques at Guantánamo. So if what you're talking about is whether *Guantánamo* is accurate, is our picture of Guantánamo accurate? Yes, it is. I don't think anyone is saying, "We don't do that, it's not what we do, we didn't do that." This is all easily checkable. The more difficult area is between the arrival in Pakistan and being picked up by the Americans. We know from documents that they arrived in Pakistan when they said they did. They weren't there for months before. They arrived in Pakistan. Within a week they'd gone to Afghanistan. They were in Afghanistan for six weeks before they were picked up. What could be in dispute is what happened to them there. What they say in the story and what we show in the film is that they ended up in Kunduz. Kunduz was surrounded by the Northern Alliance, and when the Taliban surrendered to the Northern Alliance, that's when they came out of Kunduz with the Taliban. That—from George Bush's point of view, or from Donald Rumsfeld's point of view—is probably reason enough for them to be in Guantánamo. I spoke to the American interrogator who was running their interrogations in Kandahar, the person deciding should they go to Guantánamo or not. And his position was, basically, if you're a foreigner and you're in Afghanistan, and you're picked up, you're going to Guantánamo. It was as if you would go there, or somewhere else. There wasn't somewhere else. You go to Guantánamo. So there really isn't that much debate. I think the one issue that people perhaps will always come back to is, why did they go? They went to Pakistan for a wedding. They went to a mosque. The guy said, you should all support your Muslim brothers in Afghanistan, and they decided to go. You can never prove motive. You certainly can't cross-check what their motive was. They were teenagers, incredibly young, naïve teenagers. Maybe they were thinking, this will be exciting, it will be an adventure. What they say is that they went there to do charity work. They went to help out people who were being bombed, or were about to be bombed. So they went along to do whatever they could to help those people. I was in Pakistan at the time. I was in Peshawar, which is near the border, and everyone there at the time would have had that opinion, that it was your duty to help the people in whatever way you could. And I think that there's quite a racist assumption going on, which says, "That's preposterous." If you think about it, during the Bosnian War, a lot of British people went over there to do charity work, just ordinary people from Britain thought, "This is terrible, what's happening, why not support and help these people." And they went over, they gave them clothes, whatever. No one thought at the time that, if you go to Bosnia, you must be a fighter, you've gone to Bosnia to help. That's ridiculous, "You've obviously gone there to fight." And I think that there is an underlying assumption in some questions journalists ask: "These guys, they couldn't possibly be going there to do something good. They must be going there to fight."

Q: What's the advantage to working with a small crew? Obviously, you might be able to move more easily. You can shoot on those local buses, you can shoot on the street without generating a huge crowd or creating a big disturbance. I don't think you lost anything cinematically with a small crew.

A: I always prefer to shoot with as small a crew as you can get away with. The first section of the film, the traveling sequences, was just camera, sound and a few people to help with production. Obviously, when you get to things like building Guantánamo, you have to have people to build it, so the crew gets bigger. Then you're dealing with a lot of extras on scenes that you have to recreate; it's more complicated, so you need more people to handle that side.

Q: Was it any more than logistics that led you to shoot in Iran? Looking at the geopolitical alignment, people could wonder about all sorts of things.

A: We had to recreate the section from Kunduz onwards, the surrender from Kunduz onwards, which includes the convoy through the mountains, Sheberghan Prison, and the Kandahar air base. We had to recreate it somewhere. Britain was obviously not going to be a great Kandahar. Not only is the landscape of southern Iran similar, you also have a lot of Uzbeki refugees there. You have a lot of Afghan refugees there, and you have a lot of Pakistani people, because it's on that junction. So that was probably the only place where we could have gotten the ethnic mix for what we were doing. We had a couple of hundred people there who had to be the right mix of prisoners and also the right mix of guards for the Northern Alliance. So it was purely a practical choice. I'd been there before, with *In This World*, I'd gone through those areas. So it was a place I knew. I didn't have to scout the world, looking for a place that was similar. I knew it was similar. We have a lot of news archive footage from that area for the story. I knew from that, having been there before, that it would match. So in the film you get archive footage and the stuff we did ourselves, and it matches pretty well spot on.

Q: How did you deal with permits to shoot under those circumstances? In Iran, Jafar Panahi shoots without permits in the street in order to avoid any interference from the government, and also presumably to avoid being required officially to submit his scripts for government review.

A: In Pakistan, we didn't have permits, because we were traveling around in such a small way, so the whole section in Pakistan we just did on the hoof, really. We had a little bit of a problem around the border. In Afghanistan, we did tell people what we were doing, and I can't remember having any problems. Filming in Afghanistan was quite straightforward, but we didn't do a huge amount there. In Iran, the situation is that as long as it's not about Iran, they don't mind. If we had said to them that we were making a film about Iran, even if it had been an innocuous film about Iran, I think they would have wanted to have known what it was. Apart from having to convince them that what we were doing was about Guantánamo, there wasn't then, "Well, what are you saying about Guantánamo?" They don't care what we're saying, as long as we're not doing something about Iran. Obviously, if it is about Iran, then you would have to show what's going on. On *In This World*, in Iran, we did have to explain what the story was to them.

Q: How cooperative was the U.S. in providing archival footage for you?

A: We did contact them about the possibility of filming there [in Guantánamo], and journalists can get some access, but when you talk to people about what the access is, it's not like you can go in and have some sort of direct communication with prisoners. It's very limited access. So it quickly became clear that there wasn't much point to us going, because we had the archive from news footage. But they did supply a lot of U.S. Department of Defense video material, showing us exactly how the cages were, so we could build the replica, and they were perfectly cooperative about that.

Q: Did you have to pay rights to Eminem for what sounded like his music that was used during one of the torture sequences in the film?

A: No, we didn't use any of Eminem's music, although we did pay rights. But Clive Stafford-Smith, the lawyer for our guys, was joking about it, because they do use Eminem along with a lot of other music. He was joking that he'd have more chance winning a case—of being able to sue the American government for copyright breach—than he would over human rights for compensation. He'd be better off representing Eminem over having his music played at Guantánamo.

Q: I understand that you had some problems with your poster, over the depiction of a prisoner wearing a hood, and over a quote from Michael Moore suggesting that every American should go and see the film.

A: In the original poster, there was the head of a prisoner and the head had a bag over it. Apparently, the MPAA, I think, said you can't show someone with a bag over his head because that would be too scary, or something. Then, there was also a Michael Moore quote which did say that "every American should see this film." There were objections to that, because children shouldn't be allowed to go see it. It seemed like such nitpicking. I can't believe there haven't been scarier posters than a man with a bag over his head.

Q: Since February, there has been an intense focus on Guantánamo. Lawyers have moved into the debate, politicians have denounced the prison and the detention of prisoners without rights. How do you see the film fitting into this? Did you inspire the groundswell of condemnations, which now seems to include Tony Blair, or do you now feel yourself to be overtaken by events, reporting old news?

A: Part of the motive of the film was to remind people that Guantánamo exists. Hopefully, you'll watch the film and feel that Guantánamo shouldn't exist and people shouldn't be treated like that. On the timing side, we showed it in Berlin, and we got a lot of coverage, especially in Europe, so even if you didn't see the film, at least you read a lot more articles about Guantánamo because there was so much coverage of it. By the time that we showed it in England—on television—there had been no criticisms of Guantánamo by government officials. Since then, the highest legal officials in Britain have said they think it should close— apparently, Tony Blair, in private, thinks it should close.

Q: He seems to think a lot of things in private.

A: I know. He doesn't want to upset anyone, obviously. So that was good. It's obviously not because of the film, but I don't care why people close it down, as long as they close it down. Apparently, George Bush also thinks it should close now, and if that's being overtaken by events, good—I hope events move swiftly and that we're rapidly taken over by events.

Q: George Bush also now thinks that we're too dependent on automobiles.

A: He's a reformed character, that George Bush.

Q: Maybe if he spent some time under torture, he would have been reformed and reached what he now thinks is the right decision even faster.

A: Americans don't think that's torture. America thinks those are legitimate interrogation techniques. All the things that you see in the film are the things that are officially committed as part of the process of interrogation. Apart from everything else, the prisoners should be prisoners of war. If America picked them up and said they were fighting in the war in Afghanistan, why aren't they prisoners of war? Why aren't they covered by the Geneva Convention? Under that Geneva Convention, they wouldn't be allowed to be interrogated at all. All they have to do is provide the basic information. You're not allowed to create systems of encouraging people to give more and more intelligence.

Q: What have people on the Right said about the film?

A: The strategy in England was to say, "I don't believe that they went there for charity work. They obviously went there to fight." Apart from anything else, leaving aside whether that's true—and how could anyone possibly know?—the point is that in the film we show that they were with the Taliban when they surrendered. From a hard-line point of view, people in the administration could say, "That is it. We don't need to know any more. They were in Afghanistan. They were with the Taliban when they surrendered. Therefore, they're going to Guantánamo." If you don't believe what they're saying, fine. But, even so, let's imagine they were there with the Taliban. Imagine that they had a rifle in their hands, which they absolutely categorically say they never had. Then what? Does that make Guantánamo right? Basically, the strategy of the Right was not to talk about Guantánamo at all, and to say that "I can't believe that anyone could be so foolish and stupid to believe that they could be in Afghanistan to do good work." And, as I've said, that's the most racist kind of underlying assumption. So, if a British guy goes to Bosnia to help out, he's doing charity work; in the thirties, people went to Spain, they were idealists doing the right thing. But if you're young and Muslim and you go to Afghanistan, you must be a terrorist.

Michael Winterbottom Opens His *Heart*

Peter Sobczynski/2007

From *eFilmCritic*, 22 June 2007. Reprinted by permission.

In recent years, British director Michael Winterbottom has made a reputation for himself as one of the most prolific filmmakers working today—and one of the most eclectic. Since 1995, he has made fifteen feature films (with three more in pre-production), including literary adaptations (*Jude*), melodramas (*Welcome to Sarajevo*), sci-fi (*Code 46*), surreal comedies (*Tristram Shandy*), erotica (*9 Songs*), biopics (*24-Hour Party People*), meditations on the war in Iraq (*In This World* and *The Road to Guantánamo*) and even a sort-of western (the brilliant and sadly underseen 2000 masterpiece *The Claim*). All of these are oddball genre choices to be sure, but with his latest work, *A Mighty Heart*, he has thrown fans perhaps his biggest curveball to date—a major studio (okay, major studio subdivision) production based on a well-known story—the kidnapping and subsequent murder of *Wall Street Journal* journalist Daniel Pearl—featuring one of the biggest names in the world, Angelina Jolie, as Mariane Pearl, Daniel's journalist wife. Mariane, whose published chronicle of the events would serve as the basis for the screenplay, spearheaded the search for her husband. She received much attention for remaining cool and collected during the entire ordeal, which culminated with the shocking release of a videotape showing Pearl's beheading at the hands of his captors, and for refusing to allow her tragedy to serve as a rallying point against all Muslims.

On the surface, *A Mighty Heart* may sound like nothing more than a glorified Lifetime Original Movie in which Angelina Jolie is allowed to indulge in the kind of emotional theatrics that always go over big at Oscar time. However, that is not the film Winterbottom has given us, and *A Mighty Heart* is far better for it. Instead, he approaches the material with a documentary-like attention to detail that focuses almost entirely

117

on the details of the investigation of Pearl's disappearance, while steering away from the expected melodramatics. This approach also extends to the central performance from Jolie. Although her movie-star presence is a bit distracting in some of the early scenes, she quickly transforms Mariane into a flesh-and-blood character whose refusal to give in to the powerful emotions she must have been feeling becomes more and more understandable as the story proceeds. When she does finally have her catharsis, it is a moment she and Winterbottom have more than earned.

Recently, I, along with two other journalists, sat down with Winterbottom during a publicity trip to Chicago, where he talked about *A Mighty Heart*, working with Jolie, and the challenges of telling a story in which virtually everyone in the audience knows the ending before the opening credits roll.

Q: Over the last few years, you have been an incredibly prolific filmmaker who has worked in a variety of genres—drama, comedy, science-fiction, biopics—and you could even argue that *The Claim* is a kind of western. You always seem to come up with a new movie that you can't imagine anyone else working today might have thought of. In the case of *A Mighty Heart*, though, I can imagine other people making a film with this subject matter, and in a way, I guess that makes it even more unusual coming from you. How did you come to choose this particular subject for your latest film?

A: Most of the films that I have done in the past are ones that I have originated with Andrew Eaton, my producer, and we usually have two or three ideas going and then we make one of them. In this case, we were offered the film, so it had a different type of background. Plan B had persuaded Mariane to give them the rights and Dede Gardner, who works with Brad Pitt, had given me the book about two years earlier. I read the book and I was really impressed by it. Last April, Brad called up and asked if I wanted to do it now. They had a script but they wanted to go again because they weren't completely happy with [it]. That meant I would be working on the script and going to Pakistan and meeting all the real people in the story and shooting at the same time and that appealed to me—I like doing things all together instead of separately.

Q: You insisted on meeting with everyone who was with Mariane at the time. Why was that important?

A: Obviously, we are telling Mariane's story from Mariane's point-of-view, to a large extent, but the other people are real people as well and they were going to be in the film. We kind of had to meet them anyway to talk to them about the film and I wanted to get their versions of what happened. They all had a lot of things to say that weren't the same in Mariane's book—perhaps things that she didn't really know—and since the book was from her point-of-view, she didn't really go around much to talk to other people, apart from probably Asra, since she was involved in the writing of the book. It was great to talk to people like the Captain who were working all hours of the day outside the house on the investigation. Obviously, when you talk to different people, you get different versions of the story. When we got a difference of opinion about what happened, we went back to that person and tried to get a sense of something that they would feel was close enough to their memory of the truth in order to be accurate, triangulating any differences in order to find a point that seemed to be correct. It gave us loads of extra useful information, and we had to do it anyway to persuade them that it was okay for us to use their lives in our film. I also wanted the actors to meet them. Inside that house, there was this small group of people that came together in this very closed location and it seemed like you wanted relationships to develop over the period of filming that echoed the real relationships. Obviously, the best way to do that was to have the actors meet the real people for however long they could—they got a handle on who that person was and their version of the events and how they behaved. Will Patton had to go to Kuwait to see Randall Bennett, who flew up from Iraq to meet him.

Q: Even before you came along, was Angelina Jolie always the lead for the film?

A: I don't know about "always," but when I was offered the job, she was going to be the lead. I met Mariane briefly in Paris to start with—I think it was more for her to meet me than the other way around—and then we all went down to Namibia—Dede and Andrew, who were the producers, and myself and Mariane—to meet with Brad and Angelina there. We had about three days talking about the possible film to come from Mariane's experience. Mariane and Angelina already knew each other and had obviously talked about things before so we mostly went through details a lot. Angelina had comments on the script but as I remember, she was more asking Mariane about particular things, about what was going on, instead of saying "I think this should be in the film." It made the whole thing kind of easy because they knew each other and trusted each other, and that was important.

Q: One of the impressive things about the film is that while the basic material could have easily been molded into a standard-issue melodrama, that is not the kind of film you have made—instead, you have used a documentary-like approach that stresses the day-to-day reality of the events that you are depicting. How did you come to choose that particular storytelling approach? Was there any resistance from producers or studios who might have preferred a more straightforward melodrama?

A: No, that was one of the lucky things. When we went down to talk about the idea in Namibia, I think Dede had the idea that we would be the right people to do the film. It was Plan B's project and then it became a Plan B-Revolution co-production and they basically gave it to us to go away and make it the way we would normally work. I think Dede had shown Brad *The Road to Guantánamo* and he thought that was a great starting point for how he wanted the film to be. Given that he was picking our scruffiest and most low-budget effort right from the beginning, it was kind of clear that they wanted us to make the film with the people we normally work with and in the way that we would normally make it so that it would end up looking and feeling like the films that we normally made. Obviously, you still have the studio issue, and at the time, it was with Warners. I'm not sure how or why, but it very quickly switched to Paramount Vantage, and that was great from our point-of-view because I knew John Lesher separately from when he was an agent. By that stage, I was already on so he knew what he was getting, while at Warners, Brad would have had to persuade them that I was a good idea since I hadn't worked with them before. It was kind of lucky. If someone asks you if you would like to make the film like a movie-of-the-week, obviously no one is going to say "Yes," but when you are actually making the film, you aren't sure whether you are or not. You just try to make it as well as you can while hoping that it doesn't turn out terrible. You do what seems right.

Q: From the films you have made based on true events, you have a fierce loyalty to telling the truth. Correct me if I am wrong, but it looked to me as if Daniel Pearl was not shown in any scene in this film in a situation that is speculative—it is always something that can be confirmed, where someone definitely saw him. Why was that important?

A: There is a very speculative book out about Daniel Pearl called *Who Killed Daniel Pearl?* After we got to the point of agreeing to do the film, the first thing [we did] was to go to Pakistan and start researching, and just before doing that, I read this book. I thought that I didn't want to go to Pakistan because it seemed too scary and it also made me feel like the Pakistan government would never let us film there. It was a bit of a panic and in a way, that book is effective because you come away from it as if it was a good detective story or thriller. But it was also kind of false. Once you start speculating, you just get into this area and that was not an area we needed to get into in the film. It was so speculative, in fact, that it put me off going anywhere in that direction. It was an easy choice to make because this story is about Mariane and her experience. We followed the shape of her book through her experiences, and the people that she meets are really the people in the house. It is really about Danny's absence and not about what is going on with him. It seemed like that would be an effective way of telling the story as well. Since I had talked to all of the people who were in the house and the actors had talked to them as well, we had all this information that was cross-referenced by six or seven different people, so it seemed redundant to start making up other stuff that no one could possibly know.

Q: How did Dan Futterman get involved with the project to play Daniel Pearl?

A: Basically he came in on a normal casting call. We saw a bunch of people in New York and Los Angeles and when I met him, I thought he was the right person. It was really just meeting and talking to him—I thought he had the right kind of intelligence and personality. I think what also predisposed me towards him is that he was a writer and I liked that idea. I really admired the script that he had written and it gave me a lot of confidence in him as a person.

Q: One of the unavoidable things that a filmmaker must face in telling a story like *A Mighty Heart* is that practically everyone who buys a ticket to see it is fully aware of how the story ends. How much of a challenge was it for you as a filmmaker to tell a story along those lines, especially when the ending is as grim and tragic as the one seen here?

A: It didn't strike me as that much of a problem, but maybe it was more of a problem than I realized. I think the only thing that people really know is what happened to Danny—they know that he was kidnapped in Pakistan and then beheaded—but I'm not sure that they know anything beyond that. Let's face it, when you do a completely fictional film, you often think that it is more interesting to tell people the end and then flash back to the beginning and tell what happened up until that point. It never struck me as a particular problem that you knew what the conclusion of the kidnapping was. Really, the film is more about Mariane—her response to the kidnapping and the news of his death, her relations to the other people in the house and their relationships to the investigation outside. When I read Mariane's book, I found all that stuff interesting and I hope that people feel the same when they watch the film.

Q: In some of your other films, improvisation has played an important role. Was that part of this film or was this something that wasn't suited for *A Mighty Heart*?

A: The screenplay was taken from the book and the conversations with all of the main characters. Then the actors went off and met the characters and they would get another version of the story, along with some other material as well. Because Mariane basically stays in the house for the whole story, we had five weeks in one house and that made it incredibly easy to shoot the film in chronological order. We could start and just plod our way through, and we shot it in pretty much the same period of time as the story. As the actors began to get to know each other a little better, there was a network of relationships that was similar to how Mariane had described the house. By the time they got together for that final dinner, when Mariane is telling them not to feel bad, it really felt like they were that group of people. Within that, each day would have scenes with dialogue that would roughly tell you the information that needed to be told, but then you could chat around it for quite a long time.

Q: Towards the end, Mariane learns of Daniel's death and goes off into a room by herself to have her brief emotional breakdown after having been seen throughout the film as very calm and controlled. It is the one cathartic moment when her character gets to let everything pour out. But that is the kind of over-the-top moment usually best suited for soap operas or Oscar clip reels if it isn't done right. Can you talk about how you developed that particular scene so that it would still fit in with the tone of the rest of the film?

A: Everyone describes how Mariane never really showed any kind of weakness or emotion in the house. But they also said that when they finally found out the news, there was a huge outpouring of grief and they all pretty much described it the same way. When it came time to do it, we knew why things happened and who said what from the real accounts and we sort of blocked it out. It was obviously clear by that point, after shooting for three or four weeks, that we were trying to make sure that we didn't portray Mariane by making her too emotional. She spent the entire time trying to clamp down on those emotions. And in a weird way, from our end, that was probably harder than going through and revealing the emotions because actors don't want to come across as cold. It was then critical that we have that kind of release because once she [did], they realized what she had been keeping inside. We just blocked it out and ran through it. Angelina was completely there from take one. So after that first take, it was just a question of making sure that the cameras were in the right place so that we didn't completely fuck it up.

Q: You aren't a director who likes to repeat himself and yet this is the third film that you have made about what is going on in this region. The other two films are small stories that represent much larger ones and I guess that with *A Mighty Heart*, you could look at it as a small and intimate story that also reflects the fact that more than two hundred journalists have been killed since these events happened. Were you conscious of that as well?

A: At the time, it was shocking because it seemed to be the first of that type and it had a certain resonance because of that. If you compare this to *The Road to Guantánamo*, I think they are kind of quite similar stories—they are both individual stories of people who get caught up in the acts of 9/11 with extreme actions on both sides. It didn't seem to me that was the point for doing the film because there have been hundreds of thousands of people killed, and it doesn't really matter if they were journalists or women or children—they are all people who have died unnecessarily. In a sense, that is what gives a kind of resonance to a film like this or a film like *Guantánamo*—the way that the polarization of the two sides since 9/11 is still going on. You could take a story that no one had ever heard of and it would still hopefully have the same impact.

Q: For a film of this nature, where you are obviously imparting a lot of detailed information, how long does it take to put together a cut of the film that conveys that information without causing viewers to get hopelessly lost or bogged down in the details?

A: You just have to keep messing around with it. We finished filming in the beginning of December but between getting back from India and the Christmas holiday, we didn't really get going until the beginning of January. With editing, you can keep at it forever, so it does help in some way to have a deadline. At some point, we decided that we were going to try to get it ready for Cannes, even though we weren't sure whether we could. In the end, we were working right up until the last second before Cannes—about five months. In this case, the film had a lot of dialogue and in some of the other films that we have done in this style, they have been pretty sparse with dialogue, which is easier in a way. In this one, you have to look at the pictures and listen to the dialogue as well. For the first cut, I had to kind of wade through everything and pull out the stuff that I liked and [see] what I had. That first stage took about six or seven weeks, but after that, it got a bit quicker. The truth is that if the deadline had been August 1 instead of May 1, I would probably still be working on it. With the first four or five cuts, you are obviously making it better but at a certain point, the changes get pretty marginal—some things get better and some things get worse—and you realize that although you are changing it, you aren't necessarily making it better. On this one, we were working on it until about four days before we showed it, so it was quite a scramble in the end.

Interview with Michael Winterbottom

Alex Fitch/2008

First published on the *Electric Sheep* website, 9 January 2009. Interview was conducted 24 November 2008. Reprinted by permission.

As part of a series celebrating architecture on film, the Barbican recently screened the underrated British science-fiction film *Code 46*, which tells a tale of forbidden love in a city that is futuristic and yet very familiar. Just before he went onstage to do a Q&A following the screening, Michael Winterbottom discussed some of the film's themes and ideas with Alex Fitch.

AF: With *Code 46*, did you try to capture a particular architectural aesthetic that hadn't been seen on film for a while?

MW: No. When we were thinking of making the film it was much more about what the characters were doing, what the society was like. So it wasn't so much about trying to find a look for the buildings or a style of architecture, it was about the function of the buildings and how the city was organized. It was to do with the relationship between the city and what was outside the city, between which spaces were safe and which weren't, between the bureaucratic controls and complete lawlessness. It was more to do with those kind of ideas, which connect the story and the characters, than it was to do with looking for a particular style.

AF: One thing that's very interesting about the style of the film—in the program notes it's described as "an architectural collage"—is that you mix shots of the Jubilee Line in London with shots of Shanghai and various other cities. When you set a film in the future, predicting what things will look like is very problematic, but making a city that's "all cities" gives it a kind of timelessness.

MW: Yeah. The idea was that we're in the future, but we're not that far in the future, so we weren't trying to imagine a society that had no connections to today's society. Between the idea of making *Code 46* and actually filming it, we did *In This World*, which is a film about refugees, and to a certain extent, some of the ideas about the landscape and the organization of the story came from working on that. Also, a huge percentage of buildings in London were there fifty years ago, so if you're talking about a film set fifty years in the future, a large number of buildings from now would still be there. There's more continuity than there is change in that respect. I wanted it to be very familiar, very recognizable, very real, and not a created world on a stage or on a set, but at the same time feel like you couldn't quite pin down that it was like any particular kind of place that exists right now. That was the criterion: to find things that were interesting and made sense of the story and gave it a context, but were one step away from the real.

AF: With that sort of retro-futurism, you seem to be following in the footsteps of Ridley Scott somewhat, by retrofitting buildings and predicting things that almost seem old the first time you see them in the film.

MW: Yeah, to a certain extent, although this is different from *Blade Runner*. I think Ridley Scott's a brilliant filmmaker but he was looking for an image and a style and we weren't. We had the experience of doing *In This World* with the refugees that we had to get papers for—it was incredibly hard to get them across any border. So, the idea is that although things are difficult, and the environment is harsh, and the ozone layer is depleted so people don't want to go out in the daylight, and it is very crowded, the city kind of functions. Outside, you have a chaotic desert, and all the outsiders are trying to get into the city, so instead of having the difference between different countries, you have just "the city" and "outside the city" replicated in lots of different places. So it was about looking for places that made sense of that idea and the specifics of the story, rather than looking for a retro style. What was brilliant about Shanghai as the core of the city in the film is that you have a whole section that's only really gone up in the last fifteen years with a determined effort to look towards the future, and then you have bits of Shanghai that look like they've been there for a century and haven't changed. You have that density of population and therefore the sense of how a society organizes itself when it's packed together—Shanghai is an incredibly crowded city, incredibly full of energy, incredibly full of work; it had the sort of energy you would have if you were in the city that we were imagining.

AF: What was the genesis of the project?

MW: I've worked with [writer] Frank Cottrell Boyce quite a few times and with Andrew Eaton, the producer. Andrew, Frank, and I were talking about things to do next and I liked the idea of doing a simple love story set in the future. The starting point was that it would be very simple and have a kind of mythic connection or fairy-tale feel to it. By being in the future, you would strip out the specific reality of this year and this time and have something more generic, more universal optimistically, or more detached from a social context. That was the original idea, but when it came to developing it, it became weirdly more than we were expecting. By the time we sent the script to actors, the actors were talking about what they thought were the politics of the script in relation to the future world, what it was saying about "the state" that they were living in. They took it in a much more overtly political or social way than they would have done if it had been set in a real city. It was almost the fact that it was fictional that made them question "is that good or bad?"—the fact that some people had freedom to move and others didn't, for instance, which, in a film set today, everyone would accept as "that's how it is."

AF: I think it's interesting that a lot of science-fiction films set in modern cities seem to have unreliable narrators. Both the two lead characters in this film end up with their memories wiped because they've broken the genetic laws, and that follows in the footsteps of the replicants in *Blade Runner*, the multiple motives of Lemmy Caution in *Alphaville*, Jonathan Pryce's character in *Brazil*. Do you think that's something to do with the multi-faceted nature of cities?

MW: Maybe. I hadn't thought of it like that. The starting point was a simple love story and then transgressive love. Then you take the Oedipal myth and genetics becoming an issue, which connects the idea of what's taboo and what's not taboo. So by introducing an element of not knowing who your parents are, that creates a place where you could break a taboo without being aware of it. At the time, and still now, there was a lot of talk of genetics and artificial reproduction, and how that connects to issues of morality. These are issues that people haven't had to face before, so it was interesting from that point of view, but as we were making the film it was more about the story rather than any social issue. All the elements, like climate change or population growth or bureaucratic controls, connect to important things going on in the world today, but we weren't trying to make a film about genetics, it's more that it just connects into our story.

AF: It's interesting to see *Code 46* again in light of the other films you've made recently. In *Code 46*, Samantha Morton's character has to be shown the photographs in her album to remind her of what happened, because those memories have been taken from her. In *24 Hour Party People*, when the fictional version of the narrator meets his real self, he says, "It didn't happen like that!" And in *A Cock and Bull Story*, you have the film within a film and the actors playing versions of themselves. Is that a theme you've become very interested in?

MW: It's an area that's interesting to work in. In one way, *In This World* was creating a fictional journey to bring over two refugees, but they were nevertheless real refugees, so we had to get real paperwork to get them across and deal with real bureaucracy on how to get that paperwork. And finally, when we took them back, one of them came back over and became a real refugee! So it's fun if those areas between the story you're telling, the world where they are set and the world where you are making them, are integral and complex and have different sorts of connections with reality. It's done in a serious way in *In This World*, or in a comic way in *24 Hour Party People*, but it's still enjoyable to play in that area. I like to film on location, and the reason we shot *Code 46* that way rather than in a studio is to place characters in real situations and see what happens.

AF: It's almost like you're bringing a degree of psycho-geography to the filmmaking process by putting actors in interesting locations.

MW: Completely! You hope the places you take them to aren't just photogenic or just some kind of background, but if you get the story right you feel you understand the characters because of the world that they're living in, and you understand a little bit more about the world because of the characters. I remember when I started watching films as a teenager, watching something like *Breathless*. It's so great when you see the characters walking down the streets of Paris because on one level you can see people looking into the camera as they walk by, and you've got two main actors who don't, so you can tell the other people aren't really in the film, they just happen to be there. That makes it more real in a way because it's really the streets of Paris, and those people are really walking there! It also makes it more fictional because it makes you very aware of the camera; there are your actors pretending the camera isn't there, and there's that guy looking at the camera who knows it is there. So in a way it both intensifies the fictional and the real aspects of the film.

AF: Regarding the creation of the futuristic world, I remember when *Minority Report* came out, Spielberg said something along the lines of, "Oh yes, we hired all these scientists to come up with things that would be coming true shortly," but it all seems absolutely ridiculous. By contrast, your film is spot on with video iPods, etc.

MW: Exactly! *Minority Report* came out while we were in preparation for ours. At one point, as a joke, we were going to do this big pseudo-scientific document about all the science that we'd drawn on to make our film because *Minority Report* was completely based on that ludicrous gadget/gimmick thing. For us, it was a question of looking at the way societies work now in different places, taking some of the issues like genetics and refugees and just move one step away from that. In the opposite sort of film, it's great to watch something like *Alphaville* and just pan across a random skyline of Paris and that is the future. It's as realistic a vision of the future as you're going to get. The only leap in a science fiction direction was that Tim Robbins's character—by having this empathy virus—could sense what people were thinking, which I think is probably quite a long time off. Apart from that, it really was quite a retro story, quite a classic, conventional story about a man who goes away, meets a girl and falls madly in love with her. The initial idea for the love story was that you cannot explain why someone falls in love with this person and not that person.

AF: It's interesting that at the end of the film the other characters try to explain away the love affair by saying, "It's a side effect of his empathy virus."

MW: It is, isn't it? A side effect of being empathic. The idea at the end was that it's about two people who can't be together. They want to be together, but the reality of their worlds is that they're opposites and they become victims of the transgression, and as usual as in today's society, the man's okay.

AF: Do you have a particular interest in science fiction or did it just feel like the right world for this story?

MW: I occasionally see science-fiction films and read science-fiction books, but I'm not a science-fiction fan in the sense of reading or watching a lot of it. It wasn't even to do with dealing with issues, it was more to do with it being in a fictional world. The futuristic world allowed us to simplify the story. That was the initial impulse, that it would be nice to do a story that was very, very simple: man meets girl, falls in love, they can't be together and they end up apart. It was the idea of the fictionality of it that was appealing, and as I said, weirdly, as you go on, that fictionality can get lost in the world that you create. You have the extra problem with science fiction, "What are we supposed to understand about this world?" which is a given when you do a film set now.

Michael Winterbottom's True Stories: *The Shock Doctrine*

John O'Connell/2009

From *The Times U.K.*, 27 August 2009. © The Times, nisyndication.com. Reprinted by permission.

The Slaughtered Lamb pub in Clerkenwell, East London, is a funny place to meet Michael Winterbottom. A stone's throw from the offices of his production company, Revolution Films, it's named in winking homage to the pub in John Landis's *An American Werewolf in London*— the one on the Yorkshire Moors where everyone stops talking when the two hitchhikers walk in. Winterbottom, it quickly becomes clear, would have been no good as an extra in that scene. He cannot stop talking. Words tumble out at speed, colliding unintelligibly.

At forty-eight, the indie auteur remains boyish in appearance and manner. You sense that his enthusiasm keeps him young; also his readiness to find things funny. This last quality, essential when you work in the British film industry, may surprise some. After all, there was a time when Winterbottom's work struck a keynote of earnest miserablism. The TV mini-series *Family*, written by Roddy Doyle, left no doubt about the wretchedness of working-class life in early 1990s Dublin. His 1995 feature debut, *Butterfly Kiss*, followed a lesbian serial killer and her submissive lover as they prowled the motorways of northern England. *Jude*, the following year, was an adaptation of Winterbottom's favorite novel, Thomas Hardy's *Jude the Obscure*, in which the hero's children hang themselves.

Even *Wonderland*, the panorama of London life from 1999, a breakthrough in terms of Winterbottom's ability to seduce a mainstream audience while remaining true to his verité aesthetic, trod a delicate line between uplifting and depressing.

More recently he's proved himself to be an adept director of comedy with two Steve Coogan vehicles: *24 Hour Party People*, the rise and fall of Manchester's rave scene, and *A Cock and Bull Story*, a spry, intelligent take on Laurence Sterne's supposedly unfilmable novel, *The Life and Opinions of Tristram Shandy*.

The film that we are here to discuss is funny only if you like your comedy terminally black—oil-black, perhaps. It's a documentary, funded by More4 and co-directed with Mat Whitecross. Based on Naomi Klein's recent exposé of so-called disaster capitalism, *The Shock Doctrine*, it's a sort of companion piece to Winterbottom's 2006 docudrama about the Tipton Three, *The Road to Guantánamo* (also co-directed by Whitecross), and the stunning *In This World*, from 2002, which traced the journey of two Afghan refugees from a camp in western Pakistan to Britain.

The Shock Doctrine examines the way that the free-market policies of Milton Friedman and the Chicago School were forced through in Chile, Russia, Britain and, most recently, Iraq by either exploiting or engineering disasters—coups, floods, and wars. It's an obvious fit for Winterbottom, a left-leaning director in the tradition of his one-time mentor Lindsay Anderson. He had long been a fan of Klein's journalism and her bestselling first book, *No Logo*, though he admits that he hadn't read *The Shock Doctrine* before Klein approached him about turning a shorter film she had made into something feature length.

Klein suggests a link between economic shock (radical spending cuts, mass unemployment) and the shock therapy practiced in the 1950s by the psychiatrist Ewen Cameron, which led to the development of Guantánamo-style torture techniques. It impressed Winterbottom as "a simple and clever idea that makes you look at things in a different way." He adds: "Naomi harnesses these events, especially the connections between what went on in Chile under Pinochet and what's going on now in Iraq, which I hadn't thought of before."

There was a more personal appeal, too. Winterbottom realized after talking to his own children that their generation knew little or nothing about, say, glasnost or the Falklands conflict. His eighteen-year-old daughter (the eldest of two) was, he decided, his ideal viewer. "She's going to be able to vote for the first time at the next election," he says. "I wanted to communicate the idea that this era she's grown up in, the era of rampant free-market capitalism, the world hasn't always been like this. For her, even the Berlin Wall is prehistory. I wanted to do justice to Naomi's arguments, but for the argument to have force you need knowledge of the facts." This the film supplies through skilful use of archive footage.

It also incorporates elements from Klein's original short film: striking animated sequences of prisoners being tortured, based on the CIA's notorious 1963 KUBARK Counterintelligence Interrogation manual, intended to instruct U.S. Army specialists in coercive techniques including electric shocks and sleep deprivation.

Winterbottom makes the point that when the current economic crisis hit, many people were not aware that to be pro-Friedman was to adopt a political position: his policies, implemented first by President Reagan and Margaret Thatcher in the 1980s, were the water we all swam in. "I'm an optimist and I think this is a good time to be arguing this case because there's a possibility we could be talking about a comeback for a Keynesian model," he says. "Naomi feels differently. She thinks that the powerful people who have benefited from these changes over the years are going to hold on to them. Maybe she's right. You only have to look at Goldman Sachs paying out record bonuses."

Winterbottom is famous for his work rate. He makes about a film a year, hopping with ease between genres and continents. "With the films we originate, it's as vague as what seems interesting to us at the time. You can work on something for ages before thinking it's a project you want to make, and of course whether or not you can get the money to make it is a key filter."

A Mighty Heart, about the killing of the American journalist Daniel Pearl in Pakistan, was like this—a personal project for Brad Pitt, whose production company had developed it, and its star Angelina Jolie. The pair approached Winterbottom and the result was a rare example of the director working with a major studio, in this case Paramount.

I ask about one of Winterbottom's strangest films, *Code 46*. "There's a moment sometimes where you think something like, 'Wouldn't it be fun to do a science fiction film?'" he says. "Though actually the starting point was more, 'Wouldn't it be fun to do a really simple love story? Maybe we could borrow a mythic structure so that it has a dream-like quality? Then maybe it would help that if we put it in a science fiction context?'"

If his films have anything in common it's their tone (naturalistic, unsentimental) and visual style: Winterbottom favors hand-held cameras, natural light, and real locations. It's a way of working that Winterbottom says was inspired by his hero Ingmar Bergman: "A tight group of people, a small crew, short shoots—when I started, that was the idea, that it's good to be small and independent. As opposed to: I've made one film, now let's see if I can get loads more money to make the next film."

Only when the conversation turns personal does Winterbottom seize up. An innocuous question about his childhood provokes an icy response: "You won't get much from that. I had a very normal, boring childhood. I'm not interested in talking about personal experiences." For the record, Winterbottom was born in Blackburn, Lancashire, where he attended Queen Elizabeth's Grammar School before going on to read English at Oxford. "I was treasurer of the Film Society. We went bankrupt, so it wasn't a good start." Next, a one-year course in film-making at Bristol, where he made a ninety-second version of *Jude the Obscure*. "Marc Evans [director of *My Little Eye* and *Snow Cake*] was there at the same time. He had to collect the bucket of blood from the abattoir for the pig-slaughter scene." He is divorced from the writer Sabrina Broadbent, who is said to have drawn on their relationship for her novel about the breakdown of a marriage, *Descent*; its narrator, Genevieve, is driven spare by her director husband's absences on film sets.

One of Winterbottom's bugbears is how poorly served British filmgoers are by multiplexes. "Cinemas should be really fun to run and to go to. But the way things are it's almost more enjoyable to watch something on DVD than it is to pay £35 to take your family to the Islington Vue and queue for fifteen minutes for popcorn. It's like going to Mc-Donald's—so depressing." He wants exhibitors to work on replicating the experience of a festival, where "for some reason people will watch films they've never heard of before and the atmosphere is great and enthusiastic—like cinema should be. The Government's plan to support digital projection in multiplexes is ridiculous. They should just build a load of cinemas that are geared up for independent films."

Coming next from Winterbottom is *The Killer Inside Me*, an adaptation of Jim Thompson's noir mystery, which he shot in Oklahoma in May with Casey Affleck, Jessica Alba, and Kate Hudson. Then there's the long-mooted film of Martin Amis's *London Fields* which, he says, "all depends on getting the right woman to play [the femme fatale] Nicola Six."

At which point the barmaid turns up David Bowie's *Rock'n'Roll Suicide* to deafening levels. Winterbottom laughs and mutters, as I catch only when I play the tape back: "Good luck transcribing this."

Michael Winterbottom: *Genova*

Colin Fraser/2009

From *FILMINK*, November 2009. Reprinted by permission.

The small British town of Blackburn, Lancashire is mostly famous for two things: four thousand holes and one prolific director. Not that a young Michael Winterbottom filled his days counting to see if indeed there were as many potholes in his home town's roads as John Lennon had famously sung about in the Beatles' song "A Day in the Life" (a task completed, incidentally, by a council worker reporting on the shabby state of Blackburn's traffic system). Winterbottom had other things on his mind.

Speaking down the line from his (hopefully hands-free) car phone, Winterbottom chatted with *FILMINK* en-route to his office in London's digitally hip inner city suburb of Clerkenwell. He's an enthusiastic man whose tumbling speech suggests a brain running faster than his mouth, as it tries to keep up with his prodigious output. That's no small task given that he's directed nineteen films since 1990, as well as a number of television programs. Winterbottom has two more projects in post-production, and another two in pre-production. In between all of that, he has also found the time to have a family. Being a father, albeit an absent one (his ex-wife, author Sabrina Broadbent, documented their life in a novel about a character's failed marriage to her notoriously forgetful filmmaker husband), is part of the inspiration for his latest film, *Genova,* the story of a recently widowed man who takes his daughters to Italy for a break.

The road to *Genova* was, to continue the Beatles analogy, a long and winding one. Before the dawn of the multiplex, dirge-filled, dark-age movie shacks forced the inquiring Winterbottom to look elsewhere for entertainment. "There were only a couple of cinemas, and it was hard to see anything that wasn't mainstream," he says. "Maybe that was part of the attraction. You had to seek it out." Fresh from film school in Bristol, Winterbottom got a job in a cutting room as an assistant editor. He learned the trade, and was soon directing drama for Thames Television. The mainstream, however, was not to his taste following formative years spent running 16mm prints of new German cinema at a film club in Oxford. "That's where it all started," Winterbottom explains. "You could see that they were quite simple really: they weren't complicated films to make. The mechanics of projection are quite similar to the mechanics of filming—I got a sense of how it works."

In 1990, Winterbottom teamed up with screenwriter and fellow Thames alumni Frank Cottrell Boyce to forge what has since become a very profitable partnership. Starring *Trainspotting*'s Ewen Bremner, *Forget About Me* marked their first collaboration (they've worked together six times since), and it has all the hallmarks that make a Winterbottom film: an intimate story, a small cast, and a tight crew working on a low budget. Conflict is at the heart of a film about two Scottish squaddies hitchhiking to a Simple Minds concert in Budapest. It all goes triangular when they both fall for the same Hungarian girl. Sexual relationships such as these, and some a great deal more complicated, are often a springboard for exploring the personal, itself a measure of Winterbottom's work.

While it's easy to tease out a few recurring threads, the overwhelming commonality when discussing Winterbottom is variety. Loathe to make the same film twice, he's a director who happily tackles ideas as diverse as rock concerts and jailed terror suspects, with approaches ranging from guerrilla-styled shoot-and-run to the complexity of big-budget period drama and the suffering that entails (frost-bite in his case, on the snowbound set of *The Claim*). It's the magic of never knowing what's coming next that has made Winterbottom one of the most exciting directors working today.

Is the challenge of diversity one that excites him? After a reflective pause, Winterbottom still isn't entirely sure. "It has its problems," he says. "If you make the same film each time, then people get an idea of what you make. They have an expectation. When you make a variety of films, it's more complicated." He stops for another rare pause before continuing at a rattling pace. "It's more complicated on a practical level. It's not a conscious thing that I want to make something different each time. It seems strange, but it's hard to find ideas that are interesting enough to become a film that I want to make. Most of the films that I've made are films that we've developed. Sometimes you've got the whole idea of something that you want to work on, but mostly you've got things that you want to start with—a story idea, perhaps—and then at some point you decide that this is the next one that you want to do. It's a process of clarification until it reaches a point where we've got a film that we want to make. Then you try to persuade other people to help you make it. Then it becomes easier."

Since he's built a voluminous back catalogue to rival Hitchcock, it's difficult to imagine Winterbottom sitting on his hands, waiting for the next big idea to walk into the office. After all, here's a man who has courted Cannes (*Welcome to Sarajevo, A Mighty Heart*), turned down Hollywood (repeatedly), filmed the unfilmable (*Tristram Shandy: A Cock And Bull Story*), introduced Thomas Hardy to a new generation (*Jude*), taken unsimulated sex to the multiplex (*9 Songs*), dipped into futuristic film-noir (*Code 46*), written Manchester's Factory Records a love poem (*24-Hour Party People*), rewrote *The Mayor of Casterbridge* (*The Claim*), and lifted the lid on Guantánamo Bay (*The Road To Guantánamo*), all the while taking critics and audiences with him. Well, most of the way. It's certainly true that the sexually explicit nature of *9 Songs* raised an eyebrow or two, along with some other body parts.

Challenging the status quo, be it through content or style, is part of what makes Winterbottom's films an event. *9 Songs* is the simple enough tale of two lovers who go to concerts and then have sex. That's the kick—it was the most sexually explicit film ever to get a mainstream release in the U.K., although Australian classifiers initially decided that the public here required greater protection, giving the film an X rating (which was subsequently overturned). Winterbottom acknowledged that many people thought it would not get a certificate there either, making the project a nonstarter. He's not the type, however, to be undone by something as simple as bureaucracy. "The film had nothing to do with violence, and nothing to do with the combination of sex and violence—it was nothing other than a love story. Why can't you show that in a cinema?" he asks. Well, now you can.

It's this spirit for adventure and drive for diversity that led to films like *Welcome to Sarajevo* and *A Mighty Heart*, both shot in tense and dangerous conditions. The devastating true story of Mariane Pearl (whose husband, journalist Daniel Pearl, was abducted and killed by terrorists in the Middle East), *A Mighty Heart* gave Angelina Jolie her best role since *Girl, Interrupted*. Winterbottom sought to give the film an authenticity that could only be achieved through shooting on location in tough Pakistani neighborhoods. That's where he and his pared-down digital crew headed. The result is a scintillating film that resonates with a rare truth and one of the most heartbreaking scenes of recent years.

Next stop *Genova,* a tale of two daughters rediscovering themselves after the sudden death of their mother. It finds Winterbottom back in a tight, personal narrative and re-teamed with writer Laurence Coriat, who had brought a nuanced life and energy to their London ode, *Wonderland,* which was shot on the streets of the famous England capital. Re-employing a vérité-drama style, Winterbottom similarly shot *Genova* fast and loose on the city streets to create a similar kind of authenticity. "From my point of view, the smaller the crew the better, and the simpler the story the better," the director says. "Hand-held cameras and natural light are good. All those things make the film even more focused on what's actually happening in front of the camera. They keep it relaxed, intimate, and enjoyable." That's if you could call being focused on the misery of a mother's passing "enjoyable." Fortunately *Genova* affords moments of levity amid the family drama.

For all the benefits afforded by digital technology, Winterbottom acknowledges that the format has its drawbacks. "In the case of *Genova,* it was a difficult choice," he explains. "We could have shot it in a bigger way, on 35mm, and we still would have been able to do most of what we did. But for me, on balance, I try to choose the simplest way possible with the smallest crew possible. There's always a preference for going that way rather than going bigger. With something like *Genova,* it's a mix. For the family scenes inside, digital video is really nice. With hand-held and a small crew, the actors can feel free to do what they want to do. It's better for intimate scenes like that. It's also nice on the streets when we can wander around and shoot where we want to shoot. The downside is that Genova is a very beautiful place, and with 35mm film, there's a richness to the look that we can't get on digital. It's a trade-off."

That trade-off is governed largely by the story itself. Winterbottom's 2002 BAFTA-winning drama *In This World* followed three Afghan refugees fleeing persecution in their homeland. The director shot on digital and on the run as he traced their harrowing journey orchestrated by people smugglers across the Middle East and Europe to eventual safety in Britain. Large-scale productions like the period films *Jude* and *The Claim* called for a different response. "Sometimes there are things that you can't do if you want to make a film that forces you into more formal settings," Winterbottom explains. "If it's a period film with 35mm and a bigger crew, you end up pushed in a certain direction. If you have to control locations, and if you can't make a film in the street without closing the street down, that immediately defines the sort of shoot that you'll have."

So it must have come as some kind of excitement when the idea for *Genova* finally took hold. It's the tale of a family pressed into crisis, and a perfect vehicle for Winterbottom's preferred filming method. It's a deceptively simple tale that opens in snowbound Illinois, with kids in a car playing games with their mother (the radiant Hope Davis). It's a guessing game that requires players to keep their eyes shut, which is never a good idea in a moving vehicle, and a fair indicator that tragedy is lurking somewhere just off camera. Then it happens: the youngest daughter, Mary (Perla Haney-Jardine), covers her mother's eyes and the car crashes; their lives are instantly and irrevocably changed.

When their professor father (Colin Firth in approachable, buttoned-down mood) is offered a teaching post in Genova, he takes it, reasoning that the change will do everyone good, notably Mary, who remains haunted by the responsibility of causing her mother's accidental death. Mary's older sister, Kelly (Willa Holland), is resentful but swayed by the possibilities offered by la dolce vita. After all, the sun and beachside beauty of Genova is a long way from concrete Chicago. So they decamp to Italy, rent a house, and try to start again.

You'd be forgiven for thinking that this is starting to sound like a *Mamma-Mia*–styled excuse for some mates to holiday on the summery Ligurian coast. After all, there's a reason why the seaport is known as "La Superba." And in part, it was. The story's inspiration was born of a sprouting love affair with the city's entrancing qualities. "I was flying out of Genova," says Winterbottom, "and I found that I really liked the place. There's a labyrinthine quality to the oldtown that's beautiful but menacing as well." The idea developed over a period, with another visit to Genova and collaboration with Laurence Coriat. "This went backwards and forwards between the two of us," the director explains. "The general idea and shape of the story was from me, but we worked on it together from there."

Genova marks a departure from politically charged material like *The Road to Guantánamo*, instead opting for a story with more immediate, tangible appeal. It clearly has a lot of personal resonance for the director.

"I have two daughters, and that was part of the attraction of *Genova*—doing a story about a father and his daughters," he says. "Over a period, and after visiting the city again, and thinking about the kind of stories that we wanted to do, the idea slowly developed and took shape." Some things, however, were certain from the start. "It was always going to be about outsiders in Genova, because I couldn't make a film about Italians in Genova. Bit by bit, we had the idea that the mother died in a car crash and the family would move. Because the mother has died, the kids are vulnerable. They're lost emotionally, and they're lost in this new world where they don't understand people, and they don't understand the place. Summer in Italy is like limbo: no one's at work or at school, and there's no way of getting to know people very easily. The shape of the story came from that—but always with the idea of possible threat or danger or foreboding."

While the girls in the film are American, their father is most certainly British. Creating a bi-national family was another obvious choice for Winterbottom ("I'm British and a father"), and one that let him fully explore the ideas of alienation that are at the heart of *Genova*. "I like the idea that the father is moving them geographically, and that there's already a cultural dislocation within his family—his children are American but he's British." Fond as Winterbottom is of layered themes, this transatlantic mix dropped into the middle of Old Europe is a superb vehicle for creating something of a narrative onion for him to peel back. "Being a different nationality makes the idea that he'd take them to Italy all the more believable, because he doesn't have all those emotional ties to Chicago. He's already uprooted in one sense. There are such big changes in moving, and being a tourist in a new city, and so on. Having children myself, it's an irresistible idea."

Casting is the glue that holds any film together. Get it wrong and you've got no film. While it's reasonable to say that all roles are equally important, some are certainly more equal than others. The daughters' experiences are instrumental to the story of *Genova*, but it's their father around whom they revolve. Just as he's not known for making the same film twice, Winterbottom seldom recycles his actors, and a new lead was sought. "I wanted the father to be sympathetic, and not to be traditional," he says. "There are too many stories where parents are completely idiotic. I didn't want that. Being a dad, I wanted him to be a sympathetic character. This story was partly about his love for the children, and his need to protect them." When it comes to the sagely gentle

Briton, look no further than Colin Firth. "The father is very understated, and I didn't want him not expressing his emotions because he's British. I didn't want him to be a caricature. Colin is a very British actor, and he's a very lovely man." As one American reviewer put it, Firth gives a generous portrayal while leaving just enough room for us to fill in the gaps. "Colin was great with the children; he very quickly established a relationship which allowed them to behave like a real family." That allowed Winterbottom to get that layer of authenticity that is so crucial to the film. "I wanted the family to feel very spontaneous and natural and intimate." That's exactly what Firth gave him.

Events take on a note of magical realism when Mary's dead mother starts visiting the young girl in Genova. Distraught at having caused the accident that killed her, Mary finds solace in the local church, and soon begins to see her mother in the streets. It's a large role that demands emotional fortitude and a big range from the relative newcomer. Perla Haney-Jardine had minor roles in *Spider-Man 3* and *Kill Bill: Vol 2*, and knew her way around a set. "Perla's parents live in a small town in North Carolina, and although she'd done a bit of acting, she wasn't from one of these families that move to L.A. to be in the business. She was just a kid with lovely parents." Although Haney-Jardine had starred in a feature directed by her father (*Anywhere, USA*), it's unlikely that it had prepared her for the demands of filming with Winterbottom. "It was obviously a difficult role, and probably the heaviest in the film," the director says. "As well as missing her mum, Mary obviously feels very guilty about her death. It was tricky to find someone that young [11 years old] who could play the part. Perla had enough experience of film to understand what it was, but at the same time, she was very normal and very bright. She had all the qualities that I wanted." Haney-Jardine shares, at least on screen, a similar disposition to Firth, and this low-key quality was exactly what the director wanted. "I really didn't want her to be a weird child, totally destroyed by the death of her mother," Winterbottom explains. But Haney-Jardine did arrive on set with a secret that, if handled poorly, could have destroyed the production: she wasn't very good at crying. For a role that requires bucket loads of heart-wrenching tears, a crash course in choking was required. Suffice to say, they worked their way through the problem.

Another problem that could have undone production on the streets of Genova was the Genovese. Film crews, no matter how small, attract attention. Those that don't lock down the set are at the mercy of background gawkers, nose-pickers, and peace-sign enthusiasts irritatingly staring down the camera lens. Winterbottom's small crew and reasonably unfamiliar cast (unfamiliar to work-a-day Italians at least) had its advantages. Shooting with that guy from *Mamma Mia!* and *Bridget Jones's Diary*, however, would still be difficult to do unnoticed. "Actually, it wasn't that much of a problem," Winterbottom says. "People leave you alone if you're small enough. For *Wonderland*, we did a lot of tests because we hadn't shot like that before. We went to bars and cafes and restaurants and so forth, and just started filming. Generally speaking, people just got on with it. And that was with a film camera, not with video. For some reason, when people see microphones, they seem to get more nervous. When we're shooting in the streets, we're kind of quiet; we don't have boards, we don't have lights, and all we have is a hand-held camera. People are so used to seeing cameras these days that they don't bother us."

In fact, it was they who were doing most of the bothering. The more threatening streets of Genova are home to a large population of "sailors' friends," who were nonplussed about becoming unpaid extras. "There are a lot of prostitutes on the streets of Genova, and as soon as any of them knew that we were coming, you could hear them start running away. We'd turn a corner and just see the backs of prostitutes running," Winterbottom laughs. "We had to find someone who'd talk to the pros, and then pay them not to disappear! Maybe they thought that we were filming for the secret police."

Although *Genova* is not Winterbottom's most political film, social commentary is never far from the director's mind, and it bubbles to the surface frequently. "A lot of films deal with immigration, dislocation, and separation," he says. "It's something that a lot of people experience—think about all the immigrant families in London. There are so many people in this city who are not from London, and who come from other parts of the world. More people are used to the idea of having one culture as children, and then a radically different one as adults. All these elements come together in *Genova*."

Producing nineteen films in nineteen years is a remarkable feat. Only Woody Allen comes close. Winterbottom's rapid-fire speech suggests an indefatigable spirit that keeps him going through the long, hard slog. A sound relationship with his producer, Andrew Eaton (who has worked with Winterbottom since the mid-nineties), has made his directing life considerably easier. "As a director, you spend a lot of time trying to work out how serious people are," Winterbottom says. "I need to persuade them that it's going to happen, and I get paranoid that they're not serious. It's easy to waste a lot of time in development when no one's that committed to making the film. Whereas we have two or three projects that we really want to make, and we can focus on the one that we want to make next."

One of those is another "unfilmable" novel, this time in the form of Martin Amis's groundbreaker *London Fields*. Still in development, Winterbottom is reticent about who might star for him in this quintessentially British production. When he's pressed, you can hear the silent smile down the line. Winterbottom was less inhibited about his ongoing project, *Seven Days*. Set over a number of years, he decided to film the story in real time, allowing his actors to literally grow into their roles. Winterbottom laughs knowingly when asked what he hoped to achieve by shooting in such a complicated way. "I just thought that it would be really interesting," he replies. "Instead of using different actors for different ages, we could just shoot the same ones as they grew older. That was one of the things about *9 Songs*. We were after authenticity. It's frustrating when you do a sex scene, and you have to fake it."

That's Michael Winterbottom in a nutshell: he doesn't fake it.

Michael Winterbottom: *The Killer Inside Me*

Damon Smith/2009

Previously unpublished. Reprinted by permission of the author.

Q: Your method of adapting novels—*Tristram Shandy, Jude the Obscure, The Mayor of Casterbridge*—is not to be strictly faithful to the story or methodology of the source text. How did that play out here?

A: Well, it was the opposite, really. When I read the book, I thought that you could almost film it. The book tells its story through dialogue. Jim Thompson is a brilliant dialogue writer and plotter. And then I approached the people who had the rights, and they already had a version of the screenplay which they'd sent me. In terms of individual scenes, it was very close to the book anyway, but the order had been changed. So my approach was to go back to the original story of the book and really keep the film as accurate and as faithful to the text as possible.

Q: What themes in the novel captivated you, and which of your own did you want to incorporate?

A: I think one of the great things about the book is the pace of the narrative. Within a few pages, the story's being set up. Lou's gone to meet Joyce Lakeland, there's been a moment of violence and sex, and really from that point on, Thompson keeps the story moving so new things are constantly happening. The story unfolds incredibly fast and it was that, I think, that made me feel it would be kind of interesting to make into a film.

Q: *The Killer Inside Me* is structured as a first-person narrative told by a deranged personality. Was there something about the psychology of Lou Ford that especially intrigued you?

A: Obviously, if you read a book and want to make it into a film, there have to be lots of things you like about it. There's something about the way Lou narrates his own story that makes you feel sort of close to him, and makes you feel as well that's something going to happen to redeem him. And what's brilliant about the way Jim Thompson tells the story is you're constantly feeling that you're going to come to this moment of knowledge—and then the book ends! [Laughs] There's a great story in the middle of the [narrative] that Lou Ford tells. He's read somewhere that there was a guy who was happily married, who had a wife and a couple of children, and then he got a girlfriend in the neighboring town, and he's happy with the girlfriend. And one day they discover the girlfriend had been killed and that the wife and children had been killed as well. And as he's telling the story, he wonders, Why does someone do that? People do these things for no apparent reason, without any explanation. Newspapers are still full of stories like that, about people who seem to live normal lives, love their children and wives, and then they decide to destroy everything, to tear everything up. Lou is that sort of character. The people who he kills are quite close to him. A lot of people in the story love him, a lot of people love him despite the fact that he's been violent towards them. So there's a sense of the kind of waste that violence creates, which [anchors] the movie, rather than the psychology of why he does it. There are psychological explanations in the book, but it's more the sense of that pointlessness and waste, and the *tenderness* of the situation that attracted me.

Q: A lot of readers of Thompson's novels have seen aspects of Greek tragedy at play in his work.

A: For me, it's Shakespearean as well. There's a sense of this person who people do love, he does have this ability to inspire trust and faith. And yet, whether because of what happened in his childhood or what his father did to him, he feels worthless in a sense. When he's destroying other people, he's trying to destroy himself. He feels like he's not worthy of being happy or being loved. So you have all this kind of stuff going on. Obviously, there's a big play on fathers in the novel: the relationship between Lou and his father, but also between Lou and Sheriff Bob Maples, who's a sort of alternative father figure, and between Chester Conway and Elmer Conway, who's another bad father. There's a pattern of relationships with fathers and surrogate fathers that runs through it. So it's an incredibly rich book, you know, it's not necessarily a naturalistic novel. But it's full of human emotions.

Q: Did you ever read Robert Polito's biography of Thompson, *Savage Art*?

A: I haven't.

Q: I'm just wondering if Thompson's connections to cinema interested you at all.

A: In terms of his own writing?

Q: Yeah, his writing for Kubrick, for instance.

A: That would not be a reason for me to make a film of this book. The reason is because it's a great book and when I read it, I felt it would be a really interesting film to make, and completely different from the films I normally write. In the end, when you choose a film, it's for that reason. The material is interesting. It's not that surprising that Jim Thompson had a connection to cinema because he's brilliant at dialogue, he's brilliant at stories, and the worlds he writes about in his novels seem like worlds that would be interesting for cinema. I think with Kubrick—I'm not sure what kind of credits he got on the two collaborations [*The Killing* and *Paths of Glory*]—I think he got an "additional dialogue" credit on one. I was talking to his daughter, who came onto the set, and she was saying that, you know, he did a lot more work on it than that. So that's kind of fascinating, but it wasn't the reason for making the film, obviously.

Q: This is your second film set in the U.S. after *The Claim*, and the first based on an American writer's book.

A: Well, we shot *The Claim* mostly in Canada. We had a couple of days in the U.S., but this is really the first film we shot in America.

Q: Was there something about filming here, as opposed to locating the story and time frame elsewhere, that appealed to you?

A: Yeah, as I said before the idea was to be very faithful to the novel. The first thing we did was to go and do a tour of West Texas. And then I was told we couldn't shoot it all in Texas because of financial [strictures]. And then we went to Oklahoma, where Jim Thompson is from. And the towns there were very similar to those in Texas, but in some ways we probably had more choices for locations that were good for the 1950s. So the idea was to make it as close to the atmosphere and landscape and society of the novel as possible.

Q: In general, you invoke genre—road movies, for example—without retaining all the expected codes. Did you see yourself trying to steer clear of certain noir conventions with this film?

A: Only in the sense that from the beginning we didn't want to do a pastiche of the 1950s. We didn't want to shoot it in a particular style because of genre or the content of the story. So it's not a particularly noir-looking film. Jim Thompson is a great writer, but he's a very simple, direct writer. He's very focused on the story and the character and what's happening and why are they doing that. Really, he's writing very lean and kind of spare. So it was trying to be true to that more than [make it] look or feel like a noir fifties' film. So in that sense, perhaps, we got away from generic convention, I'm not sure. But basically, it's okay, this is how the book works, and [we said] let's find an approach to the film that will be in keeping with that.

Q: Tell me a little about how you arrived at the color scheme and compositional strategy for *Killer*. The images I've seen seem more saturated than in your previous work.

A: Obviously at the moment, we're still in the middle of making the film, so to a certain extent, these are things we're still kind of thinking about, about what the color palette should be. Before we started filming, we did tests on location, we went to the person who's transferring the rushes. So you're seeing what's really a rough-grade [print], which is what we've played around with. Obviously, you respond to the landscape you're filming, the places you're filming in. Looking at archival material from the fifties, and going to visit the arid landscape in Texas where it's set—and looking at the towns, the much more lush town squares in Oklahoma and Texas—we were trying to find some kind of palette to make sense of that. I kind of liked the idea that a lot of costumes would be quite bold colors in a very fifties' way. And then we slightly desaturated from the original colors. The original colors on the clothes are very strong, so we pulled them down a little bit and went for a slightly magenta-y bias in the shadows and a sort of yellowy bias in the highlights. So it's got a slightly kind of odd cross of colors in it. Whether that'll be exactly what we do when we get to it, we don't know. After you've watched it for a few moments, sometimes you change your mind a little bit. And obviously these days, you've got quite a lot of flexibility to mess around with it. The exteriors, you know—it was very bright and hot when we were filming—so you have these bright, kind of flat, washed-out exteriors. And then the much more gloomy, dark interiors. But all of these things come from the natural way the story is and the locations, as opposed to being necessarily imposed upon the story by us.

Q: Did you check out Burt Kennedy's previous adaptation of *The Killer Inside Me?*

A: I haven't. To be honest, I didn't realize there was a version when I read the book. I chased down the producers who have the rights and they said there was one. And by that point, because I was already hoping to make the film, I said I didn't want to be doing a remake. So I haven't seen it yet. In fact, I think I'll wait till I've finished this and then watch it.

Q: You're working with a new screenwriter and editor on this picture. How have you acclimated them to the Revolution team?

A: Well, we didn't really work on the script that much. What happened was, I went to the producers and they sent me the script. They've been trying to make the film for like ten years, so they'd had lots of versions of screenplays. They sent me John Curran's screenplay. I then reworked that on the basis of bringing it back toward the book. A lot of dialogue within the scenes and the dynamic between scenes is the same as the book. But I reorganized it to bring it even closer. And then we worked from there. So to be honest, I haven't even met John Curran. [Laughs] It's not a major transformation or adaptation. It's almost a film of the book, rather than a translation from the book. On the editing side, we're all working together, we just started, so they have plenty of time to get used to the way we work.

Q: Have you thought at all about music and the kind of mood you want to evoke?

A: A little bit. You know, we have a lot of Texas swing and pop music. We shifted the book to '57, partly for architecture and so on, and we kind of wanted a more modern style for the new aspect of the time, because the idea in the book is that Central City is a small Western town and that when the oil came, suddenly it exploded, so we have a mix of fifties' architecture for the new town and the old Western-style, turn-of-the-century architecture. The idea is to use music from the period—a lot of it from radio—so there will be a cross section of pop and some sort of Texas swing. But also in the house, we're using classical music and hopefully it would be the kind of music Lou's dad was still listening to. He still lives at his father's house and reads his father's books and so on. Added to that is he listens to his father's music, so it means using a different kind of music inside the house for his private world compared to the outside world.

Q: In the past, when you've made period dramas like *Jude* or *The Claim*, you always manage to retain a very contemporary language and feel to the way you dramatize things. Is that something you've continued here, with *The Killer Inside Me*?

A: Well, I think Jim Thompson's stories are actually very contemporary, and one of the things is that it's someone writing in the early fifties about small-town Midwest America, talking about the sex and violence that goes on behind closed doors. The dialogue we're using in the film is very much taken from the book. Even so, it feels very contemporary because when you read the novel, it's very fresh. You really don't feel you're reading a creaky old period piece.

Q: You favor a cinema without constraints, really, one of total freedom. You use radio mics and handheld cameras, you don't like relighting or overdesigning space. You just set up and shoot. Is it a mystery to you why more filmmakers don't adopt your working methods?

A: I think it depends what sort of film you're trying to make. If you're trying to make a film that's very organized and which will make clear to the audience exactly what the audience response should be at any given moment, then you can shoot in a more organized way. But I like the idea that when you start a film there's a certain amount of freedom, that the actors have a certain amount of freedom, that the camera can respond to what's happening in terms of the action rather than it all being preorganized. If you work in that way, in a more improvised manner, then the film respects that, it will have elements of that within it, so the film itself will be more open and looser. And that's a choice you have to make. It depends on what type of cinema you like to make, what type of cinema you like to watch.

Q: I was just thinking about what you've always said about working with Lindsay Anderson, and how that taught you how you *didn't* want to make films.

A: I love Lindsay's films! Lindsay's films are very bold and free, certainly in that middle period. And his documentaries are great as well. But the attitude of Lindsay's that made me [criticize] him was his lack of working. It wasn't his approach to cinema. When you look at his career, he just didn't make as many films as he should have. And that was partly to do with wanting to be engaged in private arguments and battles rather than being more focused on making films. But I love his cinema.

Q: Though I've never seen you talk about it much in interviews, and quite apart from what you achieved with *9 Songs*, I think that romance and passion are abiding concerns for you. *Butterfly Kiss* was a love story. So was *Jude* and *I Want You* and *Code 46* and *The Claim*, though in markedly different ways. Are you a romantic?

A: [Laughs] Definitely! If *Butterfly Kiss* can be considered romantic, then

I'm a romantic. [Laughs] I mean, in a way this is quite a similar story to *Butterfly Kiss*, bizarrely. There are elements of violence, someone who kills several people. But there's a tenderness as well, which is what we're trying to bring out in the film, a sense that it's the kind of serial-killer story where violence is what defines him. When you read the book, there's a place when he decides to kill Amy where you feel he could be happy with her, and obviously there's a genuine passion for Joyce. In many respects, there are many elements of a love story we're trying to make with *The Killer Inside Me*.

Q: From *Welcome to Sarajevo* to *In This World*, *The Road to Guantánamo* and the new *Shock Doctrine*, you've evinced a concern with real-world issues, though you always approach them through stories of individuals on the margins, people mired in larger sociopolitical circumstances. Do you have a special interest in journalism, or let's say, in cinema as a mode of truth-telling?

A: Obviously, there are connections between journalism and cinema in the way you make a film. Whether it's complete fiction [or not], you're making something you hope makes people think about lives throughout the world. On the one hand, there's stuff to do with society, and on the other there's stuff to do with individuals. For me, almost all stories are about people's own lives, their individual passions and hopes or whatever, and how they are formed and created and connected to the rest of society. I think journalism is the same in some ways. It makes people think about the world around them, it tries to tell them stories that help them to understand the world around them. And for me, the films you mentioned—leaving aside *The Shock Doctrine*, because that was shot as a straight documentary—the primary thing, as you said, is that the story itself . . . well, actually, there is a parallel, which is that the story has to be interesting. I don't want to make a film just about an issue, because it's important. You have to find a story you feel you can make an interesting film about. In the case of *In This World*, which partly came out of the hostile reaction in the press to immigrants trying to get into Europe—in Britain especially, a lot of the papers were very hostile to any immigrants, whether asylum seekers or migrants, entering the country at that time. So that was one of the starting points in wanting to make that film. There's also just the stories of people's individual journeys, then meeting refugees who had arrived here and then meeting those still in refugee camps trying to get here. You could tell their stories and that would be interesting. It's certainly at that point, you feel you can make a film about them. I don't want a film just about the issue of immigration. But also, with *In This World*, it was partly because I liked the idea of doing a road movie. It seemed to me it could be shot digitally, [you'd get] masses of material, and you could do a much freer road movie than perhaps you could shooting on film. It was also formally or technically interesting.

Q: Do you have plans to release *The Shock Doctrine* theatrically?

A: Well, there'd been a short made before, and the people who made it came to me and said "Let's do a longer film." And originally, we got money from TV in England. When we were halfway through it, we showed it as a work-in-progress in Berlin, and now we're going to show it at some film festivals. So it has been bought in some countries as a possible theatrical release, but probably not in the U.K.

Q: Looking back at your work, what would you say is the film you're most proud of having made?

A: I don't know, really. I don't really watch stuff once it's finished. Your memories of films is kind of a weird mix between how it was to make it and what you felt about it at the time, colored possibly to a certain extent by what the response was from other people. But I don't have an objective sense of 'Well, I think that was the best one, this was the worst one.' Some are more enjoyable, some you remember more fondly than others. Not that they were better films, but they were the ones that were most engaging at the time. We're kind of lucky in that we tend to develop our own projects, so usually with a film you're hoping, when you start, that it will be close to your heart. And sometimes it just doesn't work out that way.

Q: I read an interview with Steve Coogan in which he said you're one of his best friends, but he still isn't sure whether you come to the set with just a vague idea of what you want to do, and it all somehow works out beautifully, or whether you're actually a lot cleverer than that.

A: [Laughs] It depends on which day it is. [Laughs] With Steve, you know, *24 Hour Party People* was an incredibly enjoyable film to make. And one of the reasons was, with Steve and a lot of the other performers as well, these were people who had [a] background in improvising. They were generous with our material. Most actors draw on the material they're given, whereas comedians like Steve, they generate a lot of their own. People were incredibly enthusiastic about the music and Manchester and the period, so it was working with people who were really full of things they wanted to do and try out. So in that kind of situation, obviously you have a structure and you have a screenplay, but you also know each day you're going to get other new stuff [from the actors]. That's great, that's a really enjoyable place to be when you know people on the set are going to be inventing stuff you haven't thought of that's going to be really good.

Q: Where do things stand right now with *Seven Days* and *Murder in Samarkand*?

A: *Seven Days* is a five-year project, and we're about two and a half years through it. So it's going fine. The story is about a father who's in prison, and the four children and the mom who visit him, so it's a series of visits across five years. He's still in prison, and the children are growing up, and that's good because we shot a week with them just now. I have to say, five years is a lot longer than you think. It seems like we've been making this all our lives already and we're only halfway through it! Apart from that, it's going well. And *Murder in Samarkand*, unfortunately, I don't think is going to happen. It was going to be with Steve Coogan, because we really wanted to do something with him again. It was a comedy about torture in Uzbekistan. And probably the moment for that, if there ever was a moment for making that film, has passed.

Index

Printed in the United States
by Baker & Taylor Publisher Services